SOVEREIGN LIVING II
A WOMAN'S GUIDE TO RECLAIMING YOUR
HEART

LAURA ALFANO

Sovereign Living II
A Woman's Guide to Reclaiming Your Heart

Laura Alfano

Copyright © 2026 Laura Alfano
All rights reserved

Laura Alfano
Alfano, Inc.
Malibu, California
LauraAlfano22@gmail.com
LauraAlfano.com

No part of this publication may be reproduced, distributed or transmitted in any form or by any means, including photocopying, recording, or other electronic or mechanical methods, without the prior written permission of the publisher, except in the case of brief quotations embodied in critical reviews and certain other noncommercial uses permitted by copyright law.

For permission requests, sales to U.S. bookstores and wholesalers, or to inquire about quantity discounts, please contact the publisher at the email address above.

Library of Congress Control Number: 2025923708

ISBN – 979-8-9938449-1-6

First Edition
10 9 8 7 6 5 4 3 2 1

Printed in the United States of America

SOVEREIGN LIVING II
A WOMAN'S GUIDE TO RECLAIMING YOUR
HEART

DEDICATION

This book is dedicated to my
three beautiful children and
their children, to my endlessly
patient parents, to my irreplaceable
siblings, and Alfano, Inc. You are all
a vital part of the legacy of love
that lives in these pages.

CONTENT

PART ONE - HEALTH 1
Stagnant to Accelerating Vitality 3
Jumping Out of Bed to Entering Into the New
Day 9
Eat to Live to Live to Eat .... .15
Live to Eat to Eat to Live .... .21
Illness to Emotional Well-Being .... .27
Lifestage to Staging Life .... .33
Midlife to Middlescence .... .43

PART TWO - FAMILY 49
History Repeating Itself to Putting an End to
History .... .51
Grieving a Loss to a Celebration of Life .... .57
Surviving to Thriving .... .63
Tribal Fear to Independent Black Sheep .... .69
Sacrifice to Self-Honoring .... .75
Family Roles to Individual Wholeness .... .81

PART THREE - MARRIAGE & PARTNERSHIP 87
Communication to Understanding .... .89
Criticism to Trust & Respect .... .97
Disconnection to Devotion & Partnership 105
Quality Time & Physical Touch to Intimacy..... 111
Conflict to Compassion & Forgiveness......... 119

PART FOUR - DIVORCE 127
Unconscious to Conscious Uncoupling 129
Revenge to Peaceful Resolution 135
Blame to Accountability 141
Resentment to Radical Forgiveness 147
Rejection to Acceptance 153

PART FIVE - PARENTING 159
Parenting Begins at Birth to Parenting Begins at Conception 161
Birth Order to Balanced Being 167
Absent to Present 175
Transactional Relationship to Emotional Warmth 181
Parenting for Control to Parenting to Empower 187
Parenting Others to Parenting Yourself 193
About Me to About You 199
Lemons to Lemonade 205
Out-law to In-law 211

AUTHOR'S NOTE

Dearest Reader,

Sovereign Living is an invitation to return home to yourself. It is not about perfection or performance but about alignment, living in harmony with your truth, your boundaries, and your deepest values. This book will help you recognize where you have given away your power and show you how to reclaim it with grace, clarity, and confidence.

This is more than a story; it is a lifeline. It shares my real and raw journey through life's firestorms, sometimes running, often walking, and in certain seasons, crawling, but always moving forward. These lessons were not learned in comfort; they were earned through heartbreak, courage, and perseverance. Each one became a stepping stone toward Sovereignty, and they can become yours too.

As you turn each page, let my voice steady you and my story remind you that you are not alone. I have been where you are and perhaps where you dare to go. I am here to guide you, believe in you, and walk this path with you.

A Call to Reclaim Your Sovereignty

For a woman, *Sovereign Living* is about unlearning dependence, reclaiming power, and defining life through her own inner authority rather than societal expectation. You were born Sovereign; it is your birthright.

This series of three books is a call to reclaim your Sovereignty: *your Crown, your Heart, and your Compass.* It reminds you that you are the ultimate authority in your life and invites you to rise in your own dominion. Each chapter offers a new perspective to help you move from self-doubt to self-mastery, from external validation to inner peace, and from autopilot to intention.

Sovereign Living invites you to step fully into your power and become the creator of your own life. Here, you will stand rooted in your truth, make decisions aligned with your soul, and create boundaries that honor your energy and well-being. You will be called to release outdated beliefs, shed conditioning, and let go of the need for approval. Instead, you will learn to trust your intuition, honor your desires, and take bold steps toward the life you deserve.

What Is Sovereign Living?

At its core, *Sovereign Living* is about embodying self-governance in every aspect of your life: emotional, spiritual, physical, and mental. It means standing firm in your values and beliefs, regardless of external expectations.

It is cultivating confidence and grace through every challenge and realizing that peace and happiness are not given by others but found within the deep well of wisdom and love already living inside you.

Sovereignty means living in alignment, connected to your truth, your purpose, and your deepest desires. It is not about power over others but about self-mastery and freedom from external validation. It is recognizing your worth, embracing your potential, and allowing yourself to thrive.

How to Use This Book

This book is meant to meet you where you are. You can read it from beginning to end or open to a chapter that speaks to your current experience. There are five parts organized by theme, and each stands on its own. One chapter a day may be all you have time for, and that is enough. You will receive what you need, exactly when you need it.

Each chapter of *Sovereign Living* is designed to guide your transformation. Consider this book a trusted companion on your journey, a way to awaken the Sovereign self within.

By way of my stories, self-inquiry exercises (*Reflect / Reframe / Reconnect*), journaling prompts, and mindful practices, you will uncover truths buried beneath layers of doubt, fear, and confusion. These practices are not meant to change who you are but to help you remember who you have always been.

Through the wisdom and insights shared in ***Sovereign Living II: A Woman's Guide to Reclaiming Your Heart***, you will explore the many dimensions of love, connection, and healing that shape the landscape of your inner and outer world.

Part One: Health invites you to nurture your physical and emotional well-being, recognizing the body as a sacred vessel of your vitality and truth.

Part Two: Family guides you to honor your roots while redefining what belonging means on your own terms.

Part Three: Marriage & Partnership explores the dance of intimacy, communication, and mutual growth, helping you cultivate relationships that reflect respect and authenticity.

Part Four: Divorce offers space for release, renewal, and rediscovery, reminding you that endings can also be beginnings.

Part Five: Parenting helps you lead with compassion and wisdom, nurturing both your children and the woman you continue to become.

Each section calls you to lead with heart, healing what has been wounded, honoring what remains, and opening to love in its most Sovereign form.

Why Sovereignty Matters

In a world that feels chaotic and uncertain, Sovereignty is the foundation of peace. It is the grounding force that allows you to live with authenticity and freedom.

No matter where you are in your journey, this book will help you release the barriers that have kept you from stepping into your full potential. You do not need permission to be your most confident, authentic, and powerful self. You were born to lead your life with intention, courage, and clarity.

Everything you need already exists within you.

As Glinda said to Dorothy in *The Wizard of Oz*, "You have always had the power, my dear; you just had to learn it for yourself."

This is your time to live Sovereign, to stand in your truth, to step into your power, and to become the woman you were always meant to be.

Welcome to ***Sovereign Living***, a journey back to yourself.

Let's get started,

Laura

INTRODUCTION

Sovereign [sov-rin]
    1. **a monarch; a supreme ruler.**
       Related Words: **absolute, autonomous, unlimited, self-governing, clear, true**

The dictionary offers a strong foundation for the word *Sovereign*, but now it is time to expand its meaning to reflect the power, grace, and presence of the **Sovereign Woman** of today.

    A **Sovereign Woman** is the guardian of her Heart, the one who loves with depth, lives with awareness, and leads with compassion.

    A **Sovereign Woman** honors her body as sacred ground, listening to its rhythms, feeding it with care, and moving it with intention.

    A **Sovereign Woman** is emotionally awake. She feels deeply but no longer allows emotion to rule her peace.

    A **Sovereign Woman** brings tenderness and truth into every relationship, transforming communication into understanding, conflict into connection, and intimacy into devotion.

    A **Sovereign Woman** forgives freely, knowing that release is the path to freedom.

    A **Sovereign Woman** models self-respect to her children, teaching through warmth, empowerment, and emotional presence.

    A **Sovereign Woman** stands rooted in love, not the love that pleases, but the love that liberates.

In your Heart, can you feel the pulse of this **Sovereign**

Woman already alive within you? If not, trust that she is there, waiting beneath the noise of expectation, the ache of old wounds, and the weight of all you have carried. This book was written to guide you there. In truth, my entire life has been a journey to uncover what it truly means to embody that power.

Sovereign Living means claiming, or reclaiming, your own Heart, not just as the center of your body but as the center of your being.

Sovereign Living means tending to your health and vitality as a sacred relationship, one built on nourishment, rest, and movement that renews your spirit.

Sovereign Living means honoring your emotions as teachers, listening to what your body and Heart are asking for rather than silencing them.

Sovereign Living means transforming relationships into sacred ground for growth, communicating with kindness, resolving conflict with grace, and meeting intimacy with presence.

Sovereign Living means releasing what no longer serves, whether in marriage, family, or belief, and walking toward forgiveness, peace, and self-respect.

Sovereign Living means parenting with emotional warmth and empowerment, guiding rather than controlling, and nurturing independence rooted in love.

Sovereign Living is the art of alignment, of living in harmony with your body, your relationships, and your soul's deepest truth.

Each chapter in ***Sovereign Living II: A Woman's Guide to Reclaiming Your Heart*** offers reflection, resonance, and gentle practices to help you return to your own rhythm, the quiet pulse that anchors you in truth. These are not instructions to follow, but invitations to remember. Every insight, every story, is a pathway back to the wisdom that has always lived within you.

Because the **Sovereign Woman** does not chase love or approval; she moves from the strength of her own heartbeat. Her Heart is her home, her teacher, and her true north. When she leads with tenderness and lives with courage, she becomes the embodiment of grace itself.

Part One

HEALTH
NURTURING VITALITY, EMOTIONAL HEALING & THE SACRED CARE OF BODY AND SOUL

Health is the harmony between body, mind, and spirit, a daily devotion to aliveness. It is not found in perfection, but in presence; not in control, but in connection to the rhythms that sustain us.

In **Stagnant to Accelerating Vitality**, you are invited to awaken the energy that already lives within you and channel it with intention. By nourishing your body, balancing your mind, and honoring your spirit, you transform vitality from fleeting motion into a steady, radiant way of being.

In **Jumping Out of Bed to Entering Into the New Day**, you rediscover morning as a sacred invitation to meet life with gratitude rather than rush. **Eat to Live to Live to Eat** and **Live to Eat to Eat to Live** reveal the dance between nourishment and pleasure, reminding you that food is both medicine and memory, an act of love for the body and the soul.

Through **Illness to Emotional Well-Being**, you begin to see symptoms not as punishment, but as messages from within, the body's language of truth and balance.

In **Lifestage to Staging Life**, inspired by Rudolf Steiner's seven-year cycles, you come to understand health not as a static state but as a living rhythm. Each season of life, from childhood wonder to midlife renewal, carries its own energetic pulse and emotional invitation. You learn to honor your body as it evolves through these cycles, to move with the natural flow of change rather than resist it, and to recognize that vitality is born not of youth, but of alignment with time's sacred choreography.

And **Midlife to Middlescence** reframes aging as awakening, a renaissance of self where wisdom and vitality coexist, and where the Heart learns to lead as fiercely as the mind.

Health, in its Sovereign form, is not merely the absence of illness; it is the radiant presence of vitality, reverence, and joy for the miracle of being alive.

Together, these chapters guide you to awaken energy, honor rhythm, and reclaim balance, to rise each day with intention, nourish yourself with love, listen to your body's wisdom, and age with grace. In doing so, you discover that true health is not something you chase, but something you cultivate through harmony of body, mind, and soul.

STAGNANT TO ACCELERATING VITALITY

"Vitality is the key to not only surviving but thriving in the Aquarian Age. As yogis, we have the tools to energize, balance, and strengthen our nervous and glandular systems so that we can respond to life with consciousness, not react to life from fear."

~ Yogi Bhajan

When we hear the word *vitality*, we often picture youth: strong bodies, glowing skin, endless energy. But in the Aquarian Age, vitality isn't a birthright; it's a conscious practice. It's the outcome of how we move, eat, sleep, think, breathe, and relate. It's not about chasing a younger version of yourself. It's about choosing presence and radiance right now, in the body and season you're in.

Vitality is energy with purpose. It's not just getting through the day; it's being lit up by life.

My Story: Movement With Meaning Restores Vitality

Some of my most vibrant seasons were anchored in movement with meaning.

As a young athlete, I felt alive and focused. Later, as a mom coaching youth sports, I was energized by being in service, by moving with my children, by the joy of shared purpose.

When I wasn't moving, physically or spiritually, my energy dimmed. After a health scare that led to emergency surgery to remove a calcified kidney stone, I entered a slow and humbling recovery. I was depleted. Even basic Pilates felt out of reach.

So I started small. I discovered Yogalates, a gentle fusion of yoga and Pilates, taught by my first yoga teacher, Lisa. Slowly, breath by breath, strength returned. Eventually, I joined a Hatha Yoga teacher training, where I was encouraged to study another lineage. That's when I found Kundalini Yoga.

Kundalini Yoga is a spiritual practice that combines movement, breathing techniques, meditation, and chanting to awaken the dormant life force energy (kundalini) at the base of the spine. This powerful energy rises through the chakras, promoting balance, vitality, and expanded consciousness in body, mind, and spirit.

Something about it felt deeply familiar, like the reverence I had learned in the Catholic Church, but with added Sovereignty and agency. It was mystical, precise, and incredibly powerful. The teachers, Susan, Guru Jagat, Tej, and Guru Jas, each lit a different spark.

Kundalini gave me more than physical strength. It gave me clarity. It amplified my energy field, cleared fear, and strengthened my nervous system. I wasn't just moving again; I was magnetizing a new experience of life. More peace. Better relationships. Clearer boundaries.

I learned that vitality isn't about force. It's about flow. And when we care for our energy field, our *aura*, we begin to attract what aligns and gently release what doesn't.

Improve Inner Flow and Live with Vitality

Vitality is not a luxury; it's your natural state when you're living in alignment. But modern life can drain your energy through habits, environments, and expectations that disconnect you from your body's wisdom. This chapter invites you to reclaim your inner flow not by doing more, but by choosing to be intentional with how you nourish, move, and tend to your energy. Small rituals. Sacred choices. Big shifts.

Reflect

Reflection invites you to remember what feeling vibrant actually feels like, so you can begin to make your way back there. Often, we don't realize how disconnected we've become from our energy until we pause to notice where we're leaking it. Begin by honoring the truth of how you feel right now.

- When was the last time you felt energized, focused, and fully alive in your body and mind?
- What habits, routines, or practices supported that season of vitality?
- Where are you currently leaking energy? Is it through poor sleep, overthinking, lack of boundaries, disconnection from the body?

Journaling Prompt: *What does vitality feel like for me and what one choice could bring me closer to it today?*

Reframe

Reframing helps you shift your understanding of energy from something elusive to something within reach. Vitality isn't about perfection or youth; it's about presence. When you align with what your body needs and honor that consistently, energy flows naturally.

- Vitality isn't reserved for the young; it's the result of conscious alignment and care.
- You don't need hours a day. Just a few sacred minutes, repeated consistently, can renew your entire system.
- Your body is your temple. Your breath is your reset. Your energy is not anyone else's job; it's your responsibility and your gift.

Mantra: *I honor my energy as sacred. I choose practices that restore my natural flow.*

Reconnect

Reconnection is the act of making daily decisions that bring you back into flow, not through intensity, but through rhythm. When you nourish the core aspects of your being, you create the conditions for vitality to return. Energy is built through devotion, not pressure.

- **Choose One Area to Nourish**
  Begin with sleep, hydration, movement, or nutrition. Start small and commit to consistency.

- **Create a Morning Vitality Ritual**
  Begin your day with:
  – Gentle stretching

– Deep breathing
  – Warm lemon water
  – Spinal movement or light yoga

- **Try the Sat Kriya Practice**
  Begin with 3 minutes daily. This powerful breath and mantra (Sat Nam) practice builds energy, balances the nervous system, and strengthens inner vitality. You can find an audio option on YouTube to guide you.

- **Incorporate Aura Builders**
  These subtle but powerful practices support energy flow and inner clarity:
  – Cold showers
  – Dry brushing, an ancient Ayurvedic practice that involves using natural bristle brush to massage the skin while it is dry.
  – Chanting or humming
  – Dance breaks
  – Nature walks with intention

Affirmation: *My energy flows freely. My body is wise. I move with clarity, rhythm, and renewed vitality.*

Final Thought: Choose Radiance Over Routine

Vitality is not lost with age.
It only sleeps beneath your awareness.
It waits for your breath to call it forward.

You are not here to crawl through your days.
You are here to glow.

To rise like morning light over still water.
To move through this world with quiet reverence.
To honor your body as a sacred home.

Move as though love lives within you.
Breathe as if each inhale is remembrance.
Exhale what dulls your shine.
Nourish what steadies your spirit.
Rest not from exhaustion, but from wisdom.

Let silence become your sanctuary.
Let presence become your prayer.
Vitality is not vanity; it is devotion to living awake.

This is Sovereign Living.

JUMPING OUT OF BED TO ENTERING INTO THE NEW DAY

"Invest the first hour of the day, 'The Golden Hour,' in yourself."
~ Brian Tracy

We often hear the phrase *how you start your day is how you live your life*, and there's truth in it. The first hour of your day is your energetic imprint. It sets the tone, the pace, the vibration of everything that follows. Yet most of us give that sacred time away to emails, demands, notifications, and the needs of others before we've even taken a full breath.

Imagine reclaiming that hour. Not as another task to master, but as an offering to yourself. A quiet honoring of your body, your mind, and your soul before the world arrives at your doorstep.

My Story: Reclaiming Mornings, Reclaiming Me

For two years, I gave my mornings away.

At 7:00 a.m. sharp, seven days a week, I was on a client status call. Holidays included. My alarm blared at 6:45, and within fifteen minutes I was upright, headset on, caffeine-fueled, and already in full reaction mode. It wasn't hard work, but it was consuming. I rarely paused to check in with myself. I was efficient… and increasingly exhausted.

When I finally asked to reframe and eliminate the early morning calls, the client said no. In response, I proposed an interim step and reduced the daily morning calls to 3 mornings a week. As I expected, the short term rental sales remained strong for the next six months.

So I proposed a new solution: no more live calls, only written updates. They agreed. In hindsight, I realized that progress sometimes requires a slower, more deliberate pace, rather than pushing others to immediately adopt what I view as efficient and effective.

What came next was nothing short of life-changing.

Now, I wake with the sun, gently, without alarms. I make my Nespresso, and I carry it to the large glass sliding doors, to gaze at the ocean from the balcony. I watch the light shift, clouds soften, birds stir. I breathe. I give thanks.

Then I roll out my yoga mat. I stretch. I do squats, light core work, and small weightlifting to feel strong in my own body. I listen to voices that lift me, Brené Brown, Mel Robbins, Jay Shetty and Simon Sinek, letting their words root deep before the noise of the world finds me. Then I journal an *intention list*: how I want to feel, how I want to move, who I want to be that day.

This new rhythm, this Sovereign entrance into my day, has created space for grace. Space for miracles. Space for me.

Reclaiming the First Hour as a Sacred Act

Your morning is not just a routine; it's a statement. How you begin your day determines not just your energy, but your alignment. Too often, we wake up and immediately react to messages, to noise, to demands that are not our own. This chapter is an invitation to take back the first hour of your day with intention, peace, and presence. You don't need a perfect plan; you need a meaningful one.

Reflect

Reflection helps you become aware of the default patterns shaping your mornings. Many people start their days in reaction mode, checking phones, hurrying through routines, or absorbing others' energy before grounding their own. Morning peace isn't about time; it's about intention.

- How do you currently begin your mornings, and how do those first moments shape the rest of your day?
- Do your first 60 minutes reflect the values, energy, or life you truly want to embody?
- Are you setting the emotional tone of your day, or allowing something external (notifications, noise, urgency) to set it for you?

Journaling Prompt: *If my morning reflected my power and peace, what would it look like?*

Reframe

Reframing invites you to stop seeing morning rituals as optional or idealistic. By choosing intention over urgency, you reclaim your energy and begin your day with Sovereignty, not submission.

- The first hour of your day is not a race; it's a ritual that shapes everything that follows.
- Morning devotion is not a luxury. It's a declaration of presence, power, and alignment.
- You don't need more time. You need to be with your time, present, grounded, and intentional.

Mantra: *I begin my day with presence. I lead my energy before anything else leads me.*

Reconnect

Reconnection is the daily act of grounding yourself before the world asks you to respond. You don't need a long or complex morning routine; you need one meaningful anchor. Start small, stay consistent, and let your mornings become a practice in remembering who you are before the world tells you who to be.

- **Reclaim Your Morning with One Sacred Practice**
  Choose a single grounding act: journaling, stretching, prayer, breathwork, or simply sipping tea in silence.

- **Begin with Gratitude**
  Start with a whispered *thank you* before your feet even touch the floor. Let gratitude shape your first thought.

- **Create a Morning Altar**
  Designate a space with a candle, photo, quote, crystal, or object that grounds and inspires you. Let it hold your intention.

- **Build Consistency, Not Perfection**
  If you miss a day, return the next. Let morning

devotion become your rhythm, not a rule, not another task, but a gift to yourself.

Affirmation: *I greet the day with peace and power. My morning is my anchor. My presence is my practice.*

Final Thought: Enter Your Day as a Sovereign, Not a Servant

Enter the day like a sacred temple.
Move slowly, reverently, awake.
Let light be your first prayer.
Let breath be your first offering.

You are not here to chase time.
You are here to create it.
You are not here to answer the world.
You are here to attune inward.

The first hour is holy ground.
Let silence speak before words.
Let gratitude steady your pulse.
Let presence crown your becoming.

Choose devotion over distraction.
Choose rhythm over rush.
Choose to rise, not react.
Enter as the Sovereign of your soul.

This is Sovereign Living.

Pro Tip:

If you're a mother with young children I understand getting a daily shower can be a challenge and one hour to yourself sounds like a vacation. Each morning take the time to root in you own energy. You can do this while brushing your teeth, getting dressed or while preparing breakfast. Use these moments to move with devotion towards your self care and the care of those you love. And consciously breathe in the love and exhale the fragments of unnecessary emotional weight in your body.

EAT TO LIVE TO LIVE TO EAT

"Cooking is all about people. Food is maybe the only universal thing that really has the power to bring everyone together. No matter what culture, everywhere around the world, people eat together."

~ Guy Fieri

There are two kinds of people: those who eat to survive, and those who live to eat. Most of us move between these two, depending on the season of life, the day, and even the hour.

Sometimes we eat because we must. A protein bar between meetings. Grocery store sushi on the way to pick up the kids. Meals that keep us alive, but not always connected.

Other times, food becomes the ritual it was always meant to be: a celebration, a conversation, a memory in the making. When we slow down enough to taste, to gather, to give thanks, we're not just feeding the body. We're feeding the soul.

My Story: Nourishment Beyond the Meal

During the height of Covid-19, my youngest daughter, and my niece, Sydney, were living with me. In a world gone quiet, our days revolved around meals, especially Taco Tuesdays. It was a ritual.

Sydney chopped the peppers, onions, and mushrooms, carefully tending the skillet and flipping the mixture to ensure the spices blended evenly. Meanwhile, I arranged the garnishes including jalapeños, cilantro, shredded cheese, avocado, and sour cream, and prepared a classic Cowboy Caviar to serve alongside the green salad. A rotisserie chicken was my personal protein addition, but otherwise, it was a fully vegan affair. Maddie would arrive just in time to set the table and help with clean-up.

We'd light candles, pour sparkling water or a splash of wine, and sit together, plates full, Hearts fuller. Sometimes we'd talk. Other times we'd laugh until we cried. Always, we were present.

Years later, the tradition remains. Maybe not every Tuesday. Maybe not always with the same ingredients, but the intention and the reverence endure.

Making Meals Sacred Again

In a fast-paced world, eating often becomes mechanical, something to "get through" rather than experience. But food is not just fuel. It's a daily invitation to presence, gratitude, and connection. This chapter invites you to reframe meals as sacred rituals, whether shared or solo, that root you in your body, nourish your spirit, and restore a sense of reverence in the everyday.

Reflect

Reflection allows you to examine your relationship with food beyond nutrition, to notice the stories, memories, and energy you bring to the table. Food is a portal to connection: with others, with memory, with yourself. When you slow down and become aware, even the simplest meal becomes meaningful.

- Do you treat food as fuel, or as a ritual that deserves presence and reverence?

- What meals do you remember most vividly from childhood or adulthood? Why did those moments matter, and what energy or emotion was present?

- When you eat alone, do you honor the moment, or rush through it distracted and disconnected?

Journaling Prompt: *What is my current relationship with food and nourishment. What kind of relationship do I want to build instead?*

Reframe

Reframing invites you to recognize meals as more than physical sustenance; they are energetic exchanges. When approached with intention, food becomes medicine, communion, and celebration. Every bite can carry presence, if you choose to make the moment matter.

- Food is not just survival; it is sacred. It carries memory, culture, comfort, and healing.

- A shared meal is more than time together; it is a living ritual of love and energy in motion.

- Even when you eat alone, you can treat yourself as an honored guest. Intention turns nourishment into ceremony.

Mantra: *I approach food as sacred. Every meal is a chance to slow down, connect, and come home to myself.*

Reconnect

Reconnection is the invitation to bring reverence back to the table, through rhythm, simplicity, and presence. You don't need extravagant meals or elaborate rituals. You need a return to awareness, and a willingness to make even everyday acts feel meaningful again.

- **Designate One Meal Each Week as Ceremony**
  Choose breakfast, lunch, or dinner. Slow down. Set the space. Make it intentional.

- **Cook with Others as Connection, Not Performance**
  Invite a child, a friend, or a partner to cook with you. Not as a task, but to share, laugh, and create something meaningful together.

- **Honor Solo Meals with Care**
  Plate your food with beauty. Sit without distraction. Eat like you're your own beloved. Savor. Give thanks.

- **Set the Table for Presence**
  Unplug. Light a candle. Say a quiet blessing or a word of gratitude. Let eating become an act of living well, not just doing more.

Affirmation: *I nourish my body with presence. I create rituals that root me in joy, gratitude, and grace.*

Final Thought: Feed More Than Your Body

To live well is to eat with reverence,
not only for the flavor, but for the moment it creates.

When you slow down,
when you gather and give thanks,
you awaken something timeless within.

Food is memory.
Food is culture.
Food is communion.

Bless the hands that prepared it,
including your own.
Taste with awareness.
Savor with gratitude.
Celebrate with love.

Because when you honor food, you honor life itself.

This is Sovereign Living.

LIVE TO EAT TO EAT TO LIVE

"You are what you eat."
~ Jean Anthelme Brillat-Savarin

This timeless phrase is more than a cliché; it's a biological and spiritual truth.

Your body is built from what you consume. The foods you eat become your bones, your blood, your skin, your hormones, your thoughts. Every cell is formed, nourished, and repaired by what you put into your mouth.

We often speak about "raising our frequency"and living more intentionally, energetically, and joyfully. But you cannot ascend spiritually while treating your body like a trash bin. Clean eating is not a trend. It's a return to reverence.

In a world of processed convenience, it's easy to forget that food is sacred. Food is life. And the cleaner your diet, the clearer your mind, the stronger your immunity, and the more resilient your spirit becomes.

My Story: From Comfort to Conscious Nourishment

Growing up in a traditional Italian-American family, love was expressed through food: heaping bowls of pasta, loaves of warm bread, meats roasted for hours, and always pastries and ice cream.

I didn't question it. Food was joy. Food was family. But what I didn't realize was how much sugar and starch were hijacking my energy and mood. After meals, I would crash not just physically, but emotionally: foggy, sluggish, irritable.

It wasn't until I became a mother that everything shifted. I wanted to feel more present, more stable, more alive. Gradually, I began eliminating what no longer served me or my children. Pasta and bread became occasional indulgences rather than nightly staples. I cut back on sugar, not through willpower but through awareness. I didn't want the crash anymore. I started drinking more water, adding more greens, and listening to how my body responded.

And something amazing happened. My mind cleared. My energy lifted. I stopped chasing caffeine or sugar spikes and started tuning into the natural rhythms of my own vitality.

Today, food is still joy, but it's also medicine. It's fuel. It's an act of self-love. And when I do indulge, in an authentic scoop of gelato in Italy or a bite of chocolate at the end of a long day, I do so with intention, not guilt. Because food, like life, is about harmony, not deprivation.

Eating With Intention, Not Guilt

Food should be a source of life, not a source of guilt. But for many, eating is tangled with judgment, emotional habits, and inherited beliefs. This chapter invites you to move from guilt to intention, to eat in a way that reflects care, consciousness, and Sovereignty. When food becomes a choice rooted in self-respect, every bite becomes an act of alignment.

Reflect

Reflection invites you to notice your relationship with food beyond calories or cravings. Are your choices made from awareness or autopilot? Are you eating to support your vitality, or to satisfy emotional patterns? By observing without judgment, you open the door to gentle, lasting transformation.

- What foods give you energy, clarity, and ease and which tend to leave you foggy, heavy, or drained?
- Are you eating out of hunger, nourishment, boredom, or emotional habit?
- Do your meals reflect your highest values, health, sustainability, mindfulness, or only your momentary cravings?

Journaling Prompt: *What would it look like to eat not from guilt or control, but from love and intention?*

Reframe

Reframing allows you to redefine what conscious nourishment truly means. Eating well is not about punishment or perfection, it's about remembering your power. You are not at war with your body. You are in partnership with it. When you eat with intention, you choose to honor your energy, not just satisfy your appetite.

- Clean eating isn't restriction, it's liberation from what dulls your light.
- Every nourishing bite raises your frequency, physically, mentally, emotionally.
- Your health isn't written in your genes alone; it's shaped by the small, sacred choices you make daily, starting in your kitchen.

Mantra: *I choose food that fuels my light. I eat in alignment with love, not guilt.*

Reconnect

Reconnection is about building small, sacred food habits that bring joy, clarity, and vitality. This isn't about detoxing your life, it's about devoting to it. Let food be medicine. Let your kitchen be a temple. Let your choices flow from love for the body that carries you.

- **Start Small**
  Add one more green to your plate each day. Let nourishment be cumulative, not overwhelming.

- **Swap Guilt Foods for Grace Foods**
  Replace processed or sugary snacks with fruit, nuts, seeds, herbal teas, or homemade options that feel intentional.

- **Try One Liquified Day a Week**
  Soups, smoothies, juices, or broths, gentle on the body, rich in nutrients, supportive of digestion and clarity.

- **Hydrate Deeply**
  Keep a beautiful water bottle nearby. Drink with reverence. Hydration is not just essential, it's holy.

- **Make Your Kitchen Sacred**
  Light a candle while you cook. Bless your ingredients. Play music. Savor the process. Let each meal be a prayer of gratitude for your life.

Affirmation: *I nourish myself with reverence. My food is chosen with intention, not guilt. My body receives it with grace.*

Final Thought: Let Food Become Your Frequency

Food is not just fuel; it is frequency, it is form.
Each bite a note in the song of your becoming.
Every flavor a vibration shaping your energy,
every meal a mirror reflecting your mindfulness.

You are not what you eat; you are what you absorb.
Choose what uplifts, what sustains, what honors life.
Let your plate be an altar, your fork a prayer.
Eat slowly, breathe deeply, taste your gratitude.

When you bless your food, you bless yourself.
When you eat with awareness, you invite radiance.
When you nourish your body, you awaken your soul.
Let every meal whisper, *I am alive*.

You are the gardener and the ground.
You are the offering and the receiver.
Eat as if the universe were feeding you, because it is.

This is Sovereign Living.

ILLNESS TO EMOTIONAL WELL-BEING

"Your body is a temple, a protective shell for your Heart and soul. It requires self-respect and nurturing through touch, movement and food. A disrupted Heart and soul will create dis-ease and dis-comfort."
~ **Louise L. Hay**

Our bodies are not simply vessels that carry us, they are storytellers. Every ache, every flare-up, every illness is a form of communication, an invitation to look inward.

Louise Hay, a pioneer in metaphysical healing, devoted her life to helping people understand this sacred mind-body connection. Her book, *Heal Your Body A-Z*, maps physical symptoms to emotional origins, offering us a compassionate lens through which we can decode our pain.

When we shift from blaming the body to listening to it, healing begins.

My Story: Pain as a Sacred Messenger

I first discovered *Heal Your Body A-Z* on a snowy morning after yoga. My yoga teacher, Lisa, had it propped open on a small table beside the tea station. I picked it up out of curiosity, not realizing I was about to uncover a mirror. When I turned to the page for *Kidney Stones*, I froze. The description read: "Lumps of undissolved anger." The truth of those words hit me instantly, like recognition in my bones.

Not long before, I had undergone emergency surgery for a lodged kidney stone that left me septic and in the ICU, fighting for my life. At that time, I was steeped in heartbreak, navigating estrangement from two of my children, ending a post-divorce toxic relationship, and carrying unspoken layers of guilt, betrayal, and grief. I hadn't allowed myself to truly feel any of it, so my body did the speaking for me.

As I reflected, other memories surfaced like messages long buried. As a child, I suffered from yearly bronchitis. Each autumn, my body would ache, my lungs tighten, my breath shorten. My home was loving, but emotions were often restrained, disagreements met with silence. My lungs, the seat of grief and expression, held everything I could not say. In adulthood, TMJ returned twice. Both times, I was in situations where my truth felt dangerous, my voice suppressed. My jaw locked until I could no longer speak without pain. The message was clear: *express or implode.*

Each illness became a breadcrumb leading me back to awareness. Each flare-up, a sacred whisper reminding me that unspoken emotion always finds form. Louise Hay's emotional diagnostics gave me language for something I had long felt: pain is not random; it is reverent. It arrives as a messenger, asking us to listen, to feel, and to finally heal.

Healing the Body Through Emotional Awareness

Your body speaks the truth while your mind may be too busy, or too afraid, to hear. Physical symptoms often begin as emotional whispers. When ignored, they grow louder. This chapter invites you to see pain not as failure, but as feedback. When you learn to listen, honor, and respond with compassion, the body becomes not just a vessel, but a teacher. Healing begins where awareness and love meet.

Reflect

Reflection helps you connect the dots between your physical experiences and emotional history. The body holds memory. It absorbs what the mind avoids. Not every pain is purely physical, and not every healing is purely medical. Begin by getting curious.

- Where in your body do you experience recurring discomfort, tightness, or illness?
- What was happening emotionally, in your relationships, work, or inner life, when those symptoms began?
- Is your body carrying what your mind hasn't yet fully processed or released?

Journaling Prompt: *What is my body trying to tell me and what have I been afraid or unwilling to hear?*

Reframe

Reframing allows you to see symptoms not as setbacks, but signals. Pain is not punishment; it's a message. When you treat your body as an ally, not an adversary, you create space for healing that honors the whole of who you are: body, mind, and soul.

- Pain is not a punishment. It's a call for attention, compassion, and change.

- Your body is not betraying you; it's fighting for you. It's carrying what your mind couldn't.
- Illness and discomfort are often the final language of a body that's been asked to carry unspoken grief, rage, or stress.

Mantra: *My body speaks with wisdom. I listen with love.*

Reconnect

Reconnection is the daily act of treating your body as sacred and creating space to process the emotions stored within. You don't need to fix everything all at once. You need to begin a new relationship with your body, one rooted in trust, curiosity, and care.

- **Track the Connection**
  Start a healing journal. Each time pain or tension arises, write what you're feeling emotionally. Patterns will emerge.

- **Speak with Love**
  Offer affirmations such as:
  – "I release what no longer serves me."
  – "I am safe in my body."
  – "I am healing, gently and fully."

- **Move With Awareness**
  Try practices like yoga, breathwork, or walking meditations. Movement supports emotional release and reconnects you with inner flow.

- **Practice Forgiveness**
  Forgive yourself. Forgive others. Forgiveness does not mean you condone the harm; it means you no longer want it living inside you.

- **Create Energetic Rituals**
  Support emotional detox through:
  – Salt baths
  – Journaling
  – Energy healing
  – Meditation
  – Visualization or cord-cutting practices

Affirmation: *I honor my body as a wise guide. I release, restore, and return to wholeness, one breath at a time.*

Final Thought: Listen to the Language of Your Body

Your body is not broken.
It is brilliant.
It remembers what your mind forgets.
It carries what your Heart cannot yet say.

Every ache is a messenger.
Every fatigue, a whisper for rest.
Every breath, a bridge back to balance.

When you listen, you begin to soften.
When you soften, you begin to heal.
Healing is not about fixing what is wrong
it is about honoring what is real.

Your body is your oldest home,
your truest compass,
your sacred storyteller.

Trust it.
Thank it.
Let it lead you home.

This is Sovereign Living.

LIFESTAGE TO STAGING LIFE

"For every human being, there are moments in life when the spirit stirs within, seeking to awaken what lies dormant, to transform mere existence into conscious becoming."
~ Rudolf Steiner

Every season of life has its own frequency, its own medicine, its own invitation to grow. True health is not the absence of illness or the perfection of habit; it is the harmony of body, mind, and soul as they move through time. Most of us drift through our years reacting to change rather than attuning to it. We resist aging instead of partnering with it. We cling to what once worked, unaware that vitality asks for reinvention with each new decade. But life, like breath, was never meant to be held; it was meant to flow.

In the early 20th century, philosopher and spiritual teacher Rudolf Steiner offered a profound framework for understanding these natural rhythms of becoming. He revealed that human life unfolds in seven-year cycles, each one a sacred passage with its own lessons, challenges, and invitations toward consciousness. When we understand these stages as sacred choreography, each offering its own tempo, teaching, and grace, we begin to live with alignment rather than resistance. We stop grasping for control and start dancing with rhythm.

To live Sovereignly is to recognize that we are cyclical beings within a cyclical world. Our physical, emotional, and spiritual well-being are deeply woven into these rhythms: our own, and those of the people we love. The aging of our parents, the blossoming of our children, the shifting of our partnerships all move within their own divine timing. When we honor these parallel seasons, we live not against time, but in rhythm with it, in sync with the larger pulse of life itself.

My Story: Happy 21st Birthday, Maddie!

It was just after Christmas, and my youngest daughter was preparing to return to university for her final semester of junior year. Her twenty-first birthday was coming up on January 16, the first milestone birthday I wouldn't be with her for. So I planned a post-holiday, pre-birthday celebration, a small family send-off to honor her next chapter.

I remember laboring over what to do for her and what to get her. How could I possibly top her eighteenth birthday? A private party with a DJ at Bar Taco, that vibrant, hip Mexican spot pulsing with energy and youth. As dinner guests drifted out, her friends flooded in after the men's basketball game. The room transformed, laughter rising, music thumping, the scent of lime and sugar in the air. We danced until midnight, spinning in a blur of joy and sweetness. It wasn't just a party; it was the feeling of being young, alive, and limitless.

This time, most of her friends were already back at school, so we kept it simple, a cozy gathering at my parents' house with her cousins. I still decorated as if it were a grand affair: black and gold everywhere, #21 cutouts shimmering from the light fixtures, and streamers that caught the glow of the evening.

The best moment came when she opened her final gift, mine. I can't recall what I bought her, but I'll never forget the look on her face, or the way my nieces, Laura and Sydney, leaned in as Maddie read the card. Inside, I wrote about the seven-year life cycles and explained she was now entering her fourth, the season of becoming.

I detailed how she was leaving behind the years of instinct and identity and stepping into a new rhythm of curiosity, ambition, and calling. This is the time, I told her, when freedom begins to seek purpose, when passion starts to ask for direction, when we begin to wonder not just who we are, but who we are meant to serve.

The room fell quiet. I could feel the words land, not just for Maddie, but for all three girls. In that moment, the air seemed to shimmer with recognition. They weren't just celebrating a birthday; they were awakening to a truth that would carry them through every season to come, that each stage of life asks for more than growth; it asks for grace, awareness, and alignment with something greater.

That evening stayed with me, a reminder that when we name the seasons of life, we give them meaning. And that awareness, of where we are and who we are becoming, is the beginning of Sovereignty.

It was Rudolf Steiner, the great seer and philosopher, who first illuminated this rhythm, a sacred seven-year map of human development that reveals how the soul unfolds, season by season, from birth into wisdom.

The Seven-Year Cycles

Ages 0–7: From Oneness to Awakening Self
The first seven years are a sacred descent, the spirit learning to inhabit the body. A child begins life in total

unity with the mother, then slowly discovers "I," the miracle of separateness. Crawling, walking, speaking, the world opens like a new language. Every act of independence, from the first steps to the first "no," marks the soul's deepening embodiment. The lesson of this cycle is trust, in the body, in the earth, and in life itself.

Ages 7–14: From Innocence to Inner Strength
This is the season of vitality and testing. The child's life force takes root as they confront the first challenges to health and selfhood: the fevers, fears, and friendships that shape resilience. It is here the will to live matures, as the body builds immunity and the spirit begins to say, "I can." Emotion awakens, and with it, empathy. The lesson of this cycle is courage, to live fully, to feel deeply, and to grow stronger through the storms.

Ages 14–21: From Emotion to Identity
Adolescence ignites the fire of the astral body, the realm of emotion, desire, and imagination. Hormones surge, boundaries stretch, and the Heart swings between ecstasy and despair. It is the age of becoming, of testing ideals, exploring love, and confronting the wildness of freedom. Though often turbulent, this time teaches discernment: how to feel without being consumed, how to love without losing oneself. The lesson here is authenticity, the birth of "Who am I?"

Ages 21–28: From Freedom to Responsibility
By our twenties, the body is strong, the will fierce, and the world wide open. We chase dreams, take risks, fall, rise, and fall again. But slowly, the desire for purpose tempers the thrill of freedom. We begin to ask not just what we can do, but why. Relationships deepen, careers form, families begin. The soul starts to ground its wings in the soil of responsibility. The lesson of this

stage is integrity, learning to live not just for oneself, but in service to life.

Ages 28–35: From Doing to Becoming
This cycle invites reflection. The myths of youth begin to dissolve, and we meet ourselves in the mirror of truth. The ego softens; the soul whispers. What once defined us externally now seeks internal alignment. Many face their first major life pivot: a career shift, a deep loss, a new calling. The lesson here is self-realization, the courage to build a life that matches the voice within.

Ages 35–42: From Control to Meaning
Midlife begins not as crisis, but as awakening. What was achieved is reexamined; what was ignored rises to be healed. The call is inward, toward purpose, wisdom, and emotional truth. The lesson of this cycle is authenticity, the power to release what no longer serves and reclaim what makes the Heart come alive.

Ages 42–49: From Mastery to Mentorship
By now, the outer striving gives way to inner mastery. We become less interested in proving and more drawn to sharing. We see the beauty in imperfection and the grace in guiding others. The lesson of this stage is contribution, to offer what we've learned with humility and Heart.

Ages 49–56: From Achievement to Essence
This is the age of essence, a time to integrate, simplify, and realign with soul priorities. What truly matters becomes clear: peace, connection, and presence. The lesson here is simplicity, learning that less is not loss, but liberation.

Ages 56–63: From Outer to Inner Power
As the body begins to slow, the spirit grows stronger.

Wisdom ripens; intuition deepens. This is the age of synthesis, where life's experiences begin to form a single, luminous thread of meaning. The lesson here is grace, learning to live from being rather than doing.

Ages 63–70: From Doing to Being

In this stage, the soul rests in its own wisdom. The urgency to achieve gives way to the quiet joy of witnessing. Eldership is not about age; it's about presence. The lesson here is acceptance, honoring the perfection of the path that brought you here.

Ages 70 and Beyond: From Individual to Infinite

At seventy and beyond, the spirit loosens its ties to the material world and begins to prepare for transcendence. This is not an ending, but an expansion, the soul's return to the vastness from which it came. The lesson here is surrender, to merge once more with the great oneness, carrying the light of a fully lived life.

Integrating the Rhythm of Your Life

Awareness is the first step toward alignment. Now that you understand the rhythm of life's seven-year cycles, how each season carries its own lesson, energy, and invitation, the next step is to bring this wisdom inward. Each breath, each year, each transition is part of a sacred choreography. Your task is not to control the tempo but to dance with it.

The reflections that follow will help you locate yourself within your current cycle and honor the rhythm of your becoming, with grace, curiosity, and trust in the unfolding of time.

Reflect

Life is not a straight line; it is a spiral. We return to familiar themes, but each time at a higher octave of understanding. Reflection helps us notice where we stand in that spiral and what is calling for renewal.

Ask yourself:

- "Where am I in my current seven-year cycle?" "What lessons, challenges, or awakenings seem to be repeating in new forms?"
- "Do I resist the changes of this season, or am I curious about what it's trying to teach me?"
- "What stage are the people I love in, my children, my parents, my partner?" "How might I offer empathy rather than expectation?"

Journaling Prompt: *What season of life am I inhabiting right now? What is this chapter asking me to release, reclaim, or reimagine?*

Reframe

To live Sovereignly is to see time not as an enemy, but as a teacher. Each cycle is not an ending, but an initiation. When we align with life's rhythm rather than resist it, growth becomes gentler, and aging becomes grace.

- You are not "losing time." You are gaining wisdom.
- Every cycle invites you to shed one layer of identity and step closer to your essence.
- The same seven-year rhythm moves through those you love, reminding you that empathy and timing are forms of love.

Empowering Question: *What if I stopped fighting change and began flowing with it, trusting that each season knows exactly what it's doing?*

Reconnect

When we honor the cycles, in ourselves and in others, we return to harmony with the natural pulse of life.

- Take time this week to identify what season you are in and mark it with ritual. Light a candle, write a letter to your past or future self, or create a small altar to symbolize what's unfolding.

- Notice what cycle your loved ones are in and support their stage with grace: patience for the young, respect for the wise, tenderness for those in transition.

- Breathe into the rhythm of your own becoming. Feel how the Heart, like life itself, expands and contracts in sacred tempo.

Affirmation: *I honor the rhythm of my life. I trust each season to reveal its wisdom in perfect time.*

Final Thought: Let Life Move Through You

The most graceful way to honor time is not to resist it, but to let it move through you.

Breathe deeply in the season you are in.
Release what no longer fits.
Meet each new chapter not with fear, but with faith.

Every seven years, life whispers: begin again.
Shed, soften, awaken.
Let the old dissolve like waves returning to the sea.
Let the new rise gently within you.

Do not mourn what is passing.
Bless it, thank it, and keep walking.
You are not running out of time,
you are ripening into it.

You are the rhythm itself,
the living pulse of becoming.

This is Sovereign Living.

MIDLIFE TO MIDDLESCENCE

*"The beauty of a woman, with
passing years only grows."*
~ Audrey Hepburn

At 30 years old, I could not begin to imagine the truth held within this quote, not even for a moment. The experience of aging is a remarkable journey, both emotionally and physically. Embracing the lessons and wisdom gained along the way has allowed me to welcome every wrinkle, every imperfection, as sacred evidence: proof that I am Sovereign, dedicated to who I am, and to what I stand for.

I am no longer concerned with how others perceive me. Instead, I understand why people are magnetized to me. My value is found in my calming presence through chaos, my thoughtful actions, and my intentional words. Of course, it doesn't hurt that I inherited my mother's radiant smile.

So, what's the difference between midlife and Middlescence? In terms of age, there's no difference at all. But in terms of mindset, it's everything.

Yes, we are in the middle part of our lives, but it's the juicy middle, filled with limitless possibilities. Middlescence is not simply about parenting aging parents, planning retirement, or traveling. It's a pivotal time to restart your story. To light a fire for a second career, a new dream, or a fresh purpose.

My Story: Midlife, Reimagined With Purpose

During my time with Modern Elder Academy, where I arranged thought leaders to teach, supported Chip

Conley's speaking engagements, and co-produced a bi-weekly virtual event during COVID-19 titled The Happy Hour Show, hosted and shared via Zoom, I met Barbara Waxman, a gerontologist and coach.

Barbara and I shared much in common, both New York-raised, now living in California, with corporate management experience and children around the same ages.

But our deepest bond was our shared enthusiasm for this beautiful phase of life Barbara so brilliantly coined the term, "Middlescence".

Think adolescence, that potent, transitional stage of rapid growth, but now layered with wisdom. The gap we often overlook is that while adolescence comes with structured guidance, Middlescence typically does not.

Perhaps that's why many people seeking renewal wind up buying Porsches or chasing younger companions, when what they are really seeking is a new sense of meaning.

Barbara is passionate about transforming the narrative around midlife stereotypes. She defines Middlescence as a transitional period, typically between ages 45 and 65, marked by an increased desire to create deeper meaning in one's life.

She suggests the most important inquiry of this stage is: "Who am I now, and who do I want to become when I grow up?" Middlescence invites you to view midlife not as a crisis, but as a second adolescence, this time with the wisdom of experience guiding your every step. Can you feel that inner voice rising, whispering: *You are meant for more than this.*

Midlife as a Portal, Not a Crisis

Midlife is not the beginning of the end; it's the beginning of you. This chapter invites you to reframe the "midlife crisis" as a conscious rebirth, a sacred turning point when clarity sharpens, desires resurface, and wisdom demands expression. You are not fading. You are unfolding. Midlife isn't a crisis to manage; it's an evolution to honor.

Reflect

Reflection helps you confront and gently release the outdated narratives surrounding aging. For many, midlife was portrayed as decline, not discovery. But underneath those limiting messages are longings still alive. This season is guiding you to listen more closely than ever.

Ask yourself:

- "What messages, cultural, familial, societal, did you internalize about aging or midlife?"
- "Do you experience this chapter as something fading… or something fertile?"
- "Are there buried ideas, dreams, or desires quietly rising in you, asking for space, asking to be chosen?"

Journaling Prompt: *What is trying to be reborn in me and what do I need to let go of in order to rise with it?*

Reframe

Reframing allows you to reclaim midlife as leverage, not loss. With age comes depth, clarity, and a kind of power that doesn't seek validation. Midlife isn't an interruption. It's a sacred invitation to reimagine, re-center, and re-emerge, wiser, freer, and more you than ever before.

- You are not too late, for anything. If the desire is alive, so is the path.
- Midlife is not a limitation; it's leverage. You know more. You care differently. You're done pretending.
- This is not a crisis. This is Middlescence, the second coming of age, when you stop performing and start becoming.

Mantra: *I am not losing time; I am reclaiming truth. I rise into this season with clarity and courage.*

Reconnect

Reconnection is about aligning action with your present truth. Midlife is a threshold, and thresholds are meant to be crossed with intention. It's time to say yes to what you've put off, denied, or dismissed. Not in haste, but in reverence. This is your return to yourself.

- **Take One Bold Step Toward a Buried Dream**
  Sign up for the class. Start the project. Book the trip. Have the conversation. Launch the thing. Begin.

- **Revisit Your Younger Self**
  Look through old journals, photos, or letters. What did she dream of? What did she love? What can you now make real?

- **Create a Ritual to Honor This Season**
  – Take a solo retreat.
  – Buy a piece of jewelry that marks this becoming.
  – Write a declaration: Who am I now? Who am I becoming?

Affirmation: *Midlife is not my ending, it is my emergence. I honor who I've been and rise into who I'm here to be.*

Final Thought: Rise, Don't Retreat

Midlife is not descent, but dawning.
Your light is refining, not fading.
You are breaking open, not down.
Old shells yield to truer selves.

This season asks you to expand.
It is not meant for shrinking.
It calls you gently into shine.
Meet yourself with wonder, not judgment.

Trust the rhythm of unfolding becoming.
Let wrinkles map rivers of wisdom.
Let lessons alchemize into inner gold.
You are still blooming, still bright.

Becoming continues, radiant and alive.
Life pulses through you, newly awake.
Walk forward with grace and curiosity.
You are ripening deeply into time.

This is Sovereign Living.

Pro Tip:

Listen to Barbara Waxman's TEDxSonomaCounty talk, *The Myth of the Midlife Crisis,* or read her book *The Middlescence Manifesto: Igniting the Passion of Midlife.* You can explore her work at BarbaraWaxman.com.

Bonus Tip:

Consider a transformative week at ModernElderAcademy.com; an incredible space to realign your soul's compass alongside fellow travelers in this sacred season of life.

For inspiration, read Chip Conley's *Midlife Manifesto*. It's about a one hour read and most certainly worth the time!

Part Two

FAMILY

BREAKING PATTERNS, HONORING ROOTS & BECOMING WHOLE

To reclaim your family story is to reclaim yourself. It is the shift from carrying inherited pain to creating conscious legacy, from repeating history to rewriting it with awareness, compassion, and grace.

In **History Repeating Itself to Putting an End to History**, you awaken to the patterns passed down through generations and learn that healing one link liberates the entire chain.

In **Grieving a Loss to a Celebration of Life**, you are guided to transform sorrow into sacred remembrance, to find beauty in impermanence and peace in renewal. Here, grief becomes not a closing, but a consecration, a way of honoring what has shaped you while opening your Heart to what is still becoming.

Surviving to Thriving reminds you that family is not only where you learned to endure, but where you now choose to expand.

In **Tribal Fear to Independent Black Sheep**, you break from belonging that demands conformity, discovering that true freedom often begins in standing alone.

Through **Sacrifice to Self-Honoring**, you transmute obligation into authenticity, learning that love without self-betrayal is the highest devotion.

And in **Family Roles to Individual Wholeness**, you release the masks that once defined you, allowing each member, including yourself, to return to truth.

This passage is the remembrance that family is not just where you come from; it is where your soul chose to evolve. Each chapter invites you to move from legacy to liberation, from pattern to purpose, and from survival to Sovereign belonging.

HISTORY REPEATING ITSELF TO PUTTING AN END TO HISTORY

> *"Those that fail to learn from history are doomed to repeat it."*
> ~ Sir Winston Churchill

Albert Einstein echoed a similar truth:

"Insanity is doing the same thing over and over again and expecting different results."

These quotes raise a deeper, more personal question: Why do we allow painful patterns to continue, within ourselves, within our families, for generations?

But what if this generation, your generation, is meant to end the cycle? What if the patterns of addiction, abandonment, estrangement, or silence dissolve with you? Would you rise to that sacred call?

Breaking generational cycles is holy work. It asks for vision, compassion, and courage. And it always begins in the same place: awareness, the first light of liberation.

My Story: Healing Through Generational Awareness

When I took a step back and studied the family stories that shaped me on both sides, I saw a breathtaking and heartbreaking pattern of love distorted by grief, fear, and silence.

I thought back to the day my mother's brother died by suicide. I was a teenager, and I still remember the anguish in my mother's voice when she received the call. Her first instinct was to be with her grieving family immediately. But my father encouraged her to wait for another sibling to arrive the next morning. I couldn't bear her pain, so I offered to drive her myself.

Decades later, that cycle repeated, this time through me. I received a call that my own brother was missing. My then-husband chose to stay home with our children. I drove alone. And just as my mother had faced an untimely loss, I too experienced one. Only in my case, I was the one who found his still body.

At the funeral, my daughter stood beside me. She didn't try to fix or explain. She simply said: "Whatever you need, Mom."

There was the same mother-daughter moment of unconditional support I had seen throughout my family's history, repeating now in my own life as I faced my brother's death. In my family, women showed up instinctively in times of crisis. The men I loved, including my father and later my former husband, had never been taught how to offer that same presence, and we often struggled to find each other in the moments that mattered most.

Another painful pattern has run through my family history, where divorce often led to distance and fractured relationships between parents and children. I watched it unfold through one of my uncles, through my former husband's grandparents, then his parents, and eventually through us. After our divorce, two of my three children became estranged.

Through deep reflection and a deep commitment to my own healing, I made a vow to keep the door open, always. And with time, one of those doors began to open in return. My son and I have been rebuilding gently and lovingly, supported by the quiet kindness of his wife. When he said, "I never stopped loving you," it felt like breath returning to my lungs.

My youngest daughter, has always remained close and eventually moved to Los Angeles after graduating college. And for the child with whom my bond was once paused, we are beginning to meet again in small, sincere steps. It is a tender opening, unfolding slowly and with care. We are finding our way back to each other.

Breaking these generational patterns begins with this kind of hope: the willingness to see clearly, to love bravely, and to rebuild gently. Healing family cycles is never a single act, but a series of compassionate choices that lead us back to one another, one softened step at a time.

How to Break Familial Cycles and Rebuild Love

Family is where we often receive our first patterns of love, of silence, of sacrifice, of pain. But what you inherit doesn't have to become what you pass on. Breaking familial cycles is not about blame; it's about awareness, courage, and compassion. This chapter invites you to become a lineage-changer: someone who sees clearly, chooses differently, and rebuilds love where it was once lost. Take the assignment seriously. You are the chosen one.

Reflect

Reflection invites you to acknowledge the emotional DNA of your lineage, the stories, wounds, and beliefs that shaped your family history. What was passed down may have been unspoken, but it's not unbreakable. Healing begins when you look at the patterns with honesty, not judgment.

Ask yourself:

- "What generational patterns such as, addiction, silence, codependency, perfectionism have shaped your family story?"
- "Where do you notice those same patterns showing up in your own relationships, choices, or inner dialogue?"
- "What beliefs or behaviors might you have unconsciously inherited that no longer serve who you're becoming?"

Journaling Prompt: *What family patterns am I ready to name, release, and rewrite for myself and for those who come after me?*

Reframe

Reframing helps you see that you were never meant to carry the unprocessed pain of those who came before you. What your ancestors couldn't heal becomes your invitation, not your sentence. Through awareness and conscious choice, you become the bridge between generations: healing backward, and building forward.

- You are not here to carry the pain; you are here to transform it.
- Their limitations were real, but they do not define your capacity for love, clarity, or freedom.
- When you see the pattern, you gain the power to change the narrative.

Mantra: *I am the cycle-breaker and the love-restorer. I choose what continues.*

Reconnect

Reconnection is the act of rewriting your lineage through intentional presence. Healing doesn't always require immediate reconciliation; it requires truth, forgiveness, and a new energetic imprint. As you do your inner work, you don't just heal yourself; you ripple healing backward to those who couldn't and forward to those who will never have to.

- **Create a Family Pattern Map**
  Identify and name what's been present across generations: grief, addiction, emotional suppression, abandonment, control. Awareness is liberation.

- **Practice Forgiveness as Release**
  Forgiveness is not excusing harm; it's reclaiming your energy. Say: "I release what was never mine to carry."

- **Keep the Door of the Heart Open**
  Reconciliation may not be possible today. Still, choose not to close your Heart. Stay open to peace, even if it comes in time.

- **Speak New Truth into the Lineage**
  Say aloud or write in your journal:
  – "It ends with me."
  – "Love flows freely now."
  – "We are whole."

Affirmation: *I break what wounded us. I build what frees us. I am the one who ends the pain and restores the love.*

Final Thought: See the Pattern, End the Cycle

You were not born to repeat what broke your Heart.
You were born to see it, name it,
and choose differently.
The pain you inherited is not your fault,
but the healing you offer can become your legacy.

Be the pattern-breaker.
Be the one who turns wounds into wisdom,
who meets silence with truth, and fear with love.

You are the bridge between
what was and what will be.
The one who restores softness
where there was survival,
and presence where there was pain.

Let your courage echo through time.
Let your compassion rewrite your lineage.
Let love begin again, through you.

This is Sovereign Living.

GRIEVING A LOSS TO A CELEBRATION OF LIFE

"What would best honor the years they didn't get? That could be one way of bringing meaning to our lives without them."
~ David Kessler

Every life is a gift, an opportunity for us to love, grow, and experience. One way to truly appreciate that gift, even after the physical loss of a loved one, is to consider how life would feel if they had never existed in yours at all.

Would you trade all those memories away, even to spare yourself the pain? Most of us would agree: it was better to have loved than never to have loved at all.

Death is inevitable, part of the natural rhythm of life. Some losses are tragic, untimely, and wildly unexpected, and it is the physical absence of our loved ones that stirs our deepest sadness. But a faith in something greater, whether that be God, universal energy, or the enduring nature of love, can remind us that the soul lives on. Their essence remains. And it encourages us to live each day as if it were a sacred gift.

We often hear about the five stages of grief: denial, anger, bargaining, depression, and acceptance. But for many, there's still a lingering question: "Now what?" How do we move forward in a way that honors the life of the one we've lost?

In search of this answer, I found David Kessler's profound book, *Finding Meaning: The Sixth Stage of Grief*. His work teaches us that healing isn't just about acceptance, it's about finding meaning. It's about answering the call to live a life that celebrates the ones who came before us.

My Story: Grief Honored Through Sacred Words

For me, writing eulogies has been the most powerful tool to process grief. It is my way of curating and honoring the impact of a loved one's life, sharing their spirit, their essence, with those who remain. It becomes a celebration rather than a sorrow.

Here is an excerpt of the eulogy I wrote for my brother **Peter**, delivered at his funeral mass in June 2007:

In Greek, the name Peter means the Rock.

Unmistakably, our Peter was strong like a Rock.

When we are born, God gives us many gifts. When Peter was born, he was given the gifts of Compassion, Intelligence, and the Ability to Nurture.

His Compassion was limitless. He cared for family, friends, even strangers, never expecting anything in return.

His Intelligence was effortless, a brilliant mind with a voracious appetite for knowledge.

His Ability to Nurture was perhaps his greatest gift. Whether it was nurturing gardens, relationships, or young Hearts, Peter infused life wherever he went.

Throughout the eulogy, I shared the voices of our family, memories and moments that illuminated who Peter truly was. Watching my family smile through their tears as I spoke their words was a moment of profound healing.

In addition to eulogies, I find comfort in rituals: laying flowers at gravesites, saying prayers aloud, or simply visiting a place that held meaning for us together.

These acts tether me to their memory, creating an unbreakable thread between their life and mine.

How to Write as a Healing Ritual

Writing can be more than reflection; it can be communion. When grief lingers or memories ache, putting pen to paper becomes a sacred bridge: between the past and the present, between silence and expression, between the seen and the unseen. This chapter invites you to use writing as ritual to heal, to honor, and to remember with grace.

Reflect

Reflection invites you to pause and remember the ones who shaped you. The people we've loved and lost leave behind more than pain. They leave wisdom, habits, values, and echoes of presence. Writing allows you to reconnect with that presence in a new form, through memory, meaning, and message.

- Who are the people you have loved and lost, by death, by distance, or by time?
- What did they teach you? What still lives in you because they once lived or loved you?
- How have you carried their legacy and how have you avoided your grief?

Journaling Prompt: *What would I write if I knew they could still read it? What do I most long for them to know?*

Reframe

Reframing helps you see that grief is not something to "get over"; it's something to live with, walk with, and write through. Mourning is not a flaw in your strength; it's a sign of how deeply you were moved. Writing becomes a sacred act not of holding on, but of holding space.

- Grief is not linear; it spirals, returns, deepens. And with each return, new meaning emerges.
- Mourning is not weakness; it is a mark of deep connection and sacred memory.
- Choosing joy, laughter, or presence is not forgetting; it is honoring. Living fully is not betrayal. It is continuation.

Mantra: *I write not to let go, but to remember. I write not from pain alone, but from love that still breathes.*

Reconnect

Reconnection is the practice of writing as a living ritual, a way to transform absence into presence. You are not writing for closure. You are writing to keep open the space where memory becomes medicine, and love continues its quiet work.

- **Create a Simple Ritual in Their Honor**
  – Light a candle each week.
  – Play their favorite song.
  – Cook a dish they loved.
  – Let this small act be a gateway to remembrance, not just sadness.

- **Write Them a Letter**
  Update them on your life. Tell them what's been hard, what's been beautiful. Write what you wish you'd said or what you never had the chance to.
- **Live a Value They Cherished**
  – If they loved laughter, make someone smile.
  – If they valued kindness, extend it today.
  – If they modeled courage, take the next brave step.

Affirmation: *I write to heal. I write to honor. I write because love doesn't end; it evolves.*

Final Thought: Let Their Love Live Through You

The truest tribute to those we've lost
is not to remain buried in sorrow,
but to rise in their honor.

To smile where they once brought laughter.
To speak truth where they stood for justice.
To open your hands where theirs once gave.

Their death may have closed a chapter,
but your living becomes the next verse,
the one written in gratitude and grace.

You are their echo in motion,
their courage reborn in your breath,
their love made visible through your days.

Let your joy be their continuation.
Let your light be their legacy.
Let your life sing their name.

This is Sovereign Living.

SURVIVING TO THRIVING

"Immigrants enter the United States with dreams of a better life for themselves and their families. Rather than posing a threat to our democracy, they reinforce and enrich the values that make America the country it is."
~ *Carlos Gutierrez*

Many of us are descendants of those who made extraordinary sacrifices, leaving behind homeland, language, and certainty to build a new beginning. For them, survival was success: safety, stability, and the hope of opportunity. Their courage created the foundation upon which our freedom stands.

Yet thriving does not come automatically. It requires awareness, the courage to pause, reflect, and ask: "Am I still living by someone else's idea of success?" "Am I repeating patterns born of necessity, not truth?" To thrive is to shift from endurance to expansion, from fear to fulfillment.

We are the bridge generation, standing between what was and what can be, between scarcity and abundance, duty and desire, survival and soul. It is our sacred task to honor the resilience of those before us while daring to live with purpose, joy, and Sovereignty.

My Story: Honoring Roots, Embracing Freedom

As the child of an immigrant, and born at the tail end of the Baby Boomer era, I believed that success in life meant following a simple formula: go to college, get a job, buy a foreign car, get married, buy a house, have children, collect designer handbags, and take vacations.

That was the picture. That was the prize. And I chased it. I earned it. But somewhere in the accumulation, I realized I had confused more with meaning.

The immigrant work ethic runs deep in my family. I honor it. I carry it. But I also see now that survival isn't the finish line. It's the foundation.

Today, when I look at my children, nieces, and nephews, I feel something powerful: relief, gratitude, and hope. They still work hard, but they work differently. They believe in rest. In boundaries. In joy.

They don't equate hustle with worth. They value experiences over things, connection over perfection, and purpose over predictability.

They're teaching me what thriving really looks like: A Saturday morning spent hiking instead of scrubbing a tub or the floor. A job that fits into a life, not the other way around. The courage to say no to burnout, and yes to balance.

And as the observing adult, I've learned to step aside. Not because I don't care, but because I do. Because I know the road to thriving must be walked, not inherited. And because the greatest respect I can show my ancestors is to live not in fear... but in **freedom**.

Honoring the Past by Living Fully Now

Survival may have been the legacy of those who came before you, but thriving is the invitation you hold now. Many of us are living out inherited narratives around success, worth, and work, mistaking exhaustion for purpose. This chapter is a reminder that rest, joy, abundance, and fulfillment are not betrayals, they are evolution. You don't just honor your lineage by enduring; you honor it by expanding.

Reflect

Reflection helps you identify where you're still living in survival mode, constantly doing, pushing, or sacrificing. These patterns often stem from family beliefs or societal conditioning that equate worth with productivity. To thrive, you must first question the blueprint.

- Where in your life are you simply "getting by"? In what areas are you on autopilot, instead of intentional presence?
- Whose definition of success are you currently living and does it truly reflect your values?
- What beliefs were handed down around work, rest, money, or joy? Have you challenged them or inherited them unexamined?

Journaling Prompt: *If I were no longer in survival mode, what would change about how I live, love, rest, and lead?*

Reframe

Reframing invites you to see thriving not as a betrayal of your roots, but as their extension. What your ancestors endured was essential, but you are here to do more than just endure. You are here to create, enjoy, and redefine wealth as wholeness.

- Survival may have been their mission, but thriving can be yours.

- Thriving isn't selfish. It's the fulfillment of all they hoped would be possible one day.

- Wealth isn't just money; it's time, energy, freedom, joy, and soul-deep satisfaction.

Mantra: *I carry their strength and I expand their vision. I choose to thrive.*

Reconnect

Reconnection is about building a life that honors your lineage by exceeding its limitations. This doesn't mean ignoring the struggle; it means alchemizing it into something more whole, more honest, more you. Thriving is a form of gratitude; a celebration of all that has been survived, so something more could be lived.

- **Choose One Area to Reclaim**
  Pick one realm, health, creativity, money, relationships, and write a clear vision of what thriving looks like for *you*.

- **Block Time to Feel Alive**
  Schedule at least one act of aliveness each week: dancing, creating, resting, connecting. Let it be non-negotiable.

- **Share the Story of Survival**
  Talk to your children or loved ones about your family's legacy. Frame their survival as the seed and your thriving as the bloom.

- **Practice Evolved Gratitude**
  Be grateful not just for what they gave you, but for what you now give yourself. Your healing is the continuation of their courage.

Affirmation: *I move beyond survival. I choose to thrive with joy, purpose, and reverence for all who made this possible.*

Final Thought: Thrive in Their Honor

Your ancestors survived so you could choose.
Not just to work harder, but to live freer.
To feel joy without guilt.
To rest without apology.

To create not from fear, but from fullness.
They built the foundation; you build the future.
Their endurance was the seed.
Your expansion is the bloom.

You are proof that their struggle had meaning.
That survival was never the end of the story,
It was the threshold of Sovereignty.
So breathe deeper.

Love wider.
Rise higher.
Let your joy honor them.
Let your peace fulfill them.

Let your thriving be the prayer they had no words for.

This is Sovereign Living.

TRIBAL FEAR TO INDEPENDENT BLACK SHEEP

"The individual has always had to struggle to keep from being overwhelmed by the tribe."
~ *Friedrich Wilhelm Nietzsche*

If you grew up in a tight-knit family or deeply rooted community, you likely know the quiet but persistent pull of tribal loyalty, the unspoken codes, the expected roles, and the sacred rhythms that govern how you're supposed to think, believe, live, and love.

At its best, the tribe offers connection, safety, and belonging. At its worst, it can demand conformity at the cost of authenticity. And sometimes, belonging means betrayal, not of them, but of yourself.

The choice to step outside of inherited beliefs doesn't make you a traitor. It makes you awake.

My Story: Belonging Without Losing Self

I grew up in what I now reverently refer to as Alfano, Inc., a multigenerational Italian-American family where tradition reigned. My fathers parents and siblings lived within blocks of each other. We attended the same Catholic school. Sundays meant church, pasta and meatballs, soccer, and storytelling, all around the kitchen table.

It was safe. It was predictable. It was beautiful. But it was not Sovereign. As a child, I never questioned it. As a teen, I began to wonder. And when college arrived, curiosity carried me far from the comfort of the tribe.

It wasn't dramatic. I didn't rebel. But I began to think for myself. To explore new faiths, new friendships, and new frameworks for living. I remember my mother's quiet blessing in this: "Just let me know where you are," she'd say, not as a leash, but as a lifeline. It was her way of saying: go and know that love follows.

Now, decades later, I hold many beliefs that differ from my original tribe:

I am Catholic and appreciate the teachings of Buddhism and Kabbalah.

I believe in marriage and in divorce, when needed.

I am a capitalist with a humanitarian soul.

I believe in individual liberty, collective responsibility, and universal compassion.

I don't need to be right. I only need to be real.

I'm not here to argue. I'm here to understand.

I'm the black sheep with an open Heart, walking freely, and wearing rose-coloered glasses, guided by love and truth.

Honoring Tradition Without Losing Who You Are

Tradition can offer belonging, but it can also become a boundary. The voices of family, culture, and community often shape our early identity. But at some point, your truth may diverge from what you were taught. This chapter invites you to navigate that tension with grace: to meet tradition not with rebellion, but with honesty. You can honor your roots without being ruled by them.

Reflect

Reflection invites you to examine the tribes, family, faith, and culture, that shaped your sense of self. Often, these early communities offer protection and identity. But they can also come with unspoken rules and pressures. Awareness is where authenticity begins.

- What tribes shaped your early identity? Was it family, religion, culture, school, or social groups? What core messages did they instill?

- Where do you still feel pressure to conform in order to be accepted in your beliefs, behavior, or life choices?

- Have you ever hidden your truth, your values, desires, or doubts, just to stay in good standing with those around you?

Journaling Prompt: *Where am I still living to please the tribe and what part of me is asking to be free?*

Reframe

Reframing empowers you to see that authenticity is not a rejection of tradition, it's a refinement of it. Carving your own path doesn't mean severing ties; it means choosing truth over expectation. You can both honor where you come from *and* walk forward in alignment with who you are becoming.

- Choosing your own path is not betrayal, it's bravery.

- The "black sheep" isn't lost, she's the first to find the clearing.

- You can love your tribe deeply and still set down the parts of the script that no longer serve you.

- Authenticity isn't disloyal. It's the most sacred form of self-respect.

Mantra: *I carry the wisdom of my lineage and the freedom to write a new chapter.*

Reconnect

Reconnection is about finding a way to live in alignment with your truth while staying rooted in love. It's not about abandoning tradition entirely, it's about integrating what's true for you, now. The future you build can still be grounded in reverence, even if the rules have changed.

- **Write Your Belief Map**
  List the beliefs or roles you inherited. Then, beside each one, write what you actually believe today. Notice where they align and where they diverge.

- **Practice Soft Courage**
  Stand in your truth without needing to convince anyone. Let quiet confidence replace the need for permission.

- **Honor the Past, Live Forward**
  Thank your ancestors and communities for what they gave you and then choose to live in a way that reflects *your* deepest values.

- **Find Kindred Spirits**
  Surround yourself with people who see and celebrate your full self, not just the version they recognize.

Affirmation: *I honor my heritage with gratitude and I honor myself with truth. I belong to my roots, and I belong to my becoming.*

Final Thought: Walk Your Path Without Permission

You were not born to repeat the story.
You were born to rewrite it.
To honor the roots that raised you,
without being bound by them.

To love your tribe,
and still choose your truth.
The path of the independent soul
is not rebellion; it is remembrance.

A return to the voice beneath the noise.
A quiet knowing that belonging begins within.
Some will misunderstand your freedom.
Let them.

Your life is not an apology.
It is an offering.
The black sheep is not lost;
she is leading.

This is Sovereign Living.

SACRIFICE TO SELF-HONORING

"Self-sacrifice which denies common sense is not a virtue. It's a spiritual dissipation."
~ Margaret Deland

In some families, especially those steeped in tradition, sacrifice is often mistaken for love. We're praised for putting others first, taught that real loyalty means saying yes, staying quiet, and showing up, no matter the personal cost.

But unchecked sacrifice doesn't lead to deeper connection. It leads to depletion. And a depleted woman cannot love fully, no matter how hard she tries.

Real love does not require self-erasure. It requires self-awareness.

My Story: Self-Honoring Is Sacred Work

There was a chapter in my life where I said yes to everything.

Yes to every school committee.
Yes to every work request.
Yes to every family favor.

I wore it like a badge of honor until the badge became a burden.

I began to feel an undercurrent of resentment toward others, but mostly toward myself. I was running on fumes, still smiling, still serving, but no longer nourished. I couldn't remember the last time I had asked myself what *I* needed. What *I* wanted. What actually made *me* feel alive. The turning point came quietly.

One afternoon, after running errands for everyone but myself, I sat in my car in a parking lot and cried. Not from a specific event, but from the slow erosion of my center. I realized I was becoming a shell of the vibrant, creative, joyful woman I used to be. So I started making changes.

I began blocking out time for rest, journaling, even solitude, without apology. I rediscovered what I loved: quiet mornings, beautiful books, spontaneous beach walks. I learned to say no with kindness.

And most importantly, I began to understand that the more whole I felt, the more love I could offer without resentment, without exhaustion.

Self-honoring wasn't selfish. It was sacred.

Saying No to Others So You Can Say Yes to Yourself

Finding yourself often begins with losing what isn't truly yours to carry. Too many people confuse self-sacrifice with love and guilt with generosity. This chapter invites you to stop abandoning yourself in the name of being needed and to begin honoring your energy, your boundaries, and your wholeness. Saying no isn't selfish; it's sacred. It creates space for the truest version of you to emerge.

Reflect

Reflection asks you to notice the places in your life where people-pleasing has replaced authenticity.

When your yes comes from guilt instead of joy, the cost is often invisible but deep: resentment, depletion, and a quiet erosion of self. You cannot "find yourself" while constantly abandoning your needs to meet everyone else's.

- Where are you saying yes out of obligation, fear, or guilt, instead of love, alignment, or choice?
- Are there signs of burnout or bitterness in your closest relationships and what are they trying to tell you?
- What parts of yourself, your rest, creativity, joy, or truth, have been ignored or sacrificed?

Journaling Prompt: *Where have I said yes to others while saying no to myself and what needs to change?*

Reframe

Reframing reminds you that love does not require the loss of self. Your boundaries are not a rejection of others; they are a reclamation of you. Saying no is not just about protecting your time; it's about protecting your vitality, your voice, and your right to choose.

- Love is not measured by how much of yourself you're willing to abandon.
- Your needs are not indulgent; they're directional. They help you stay aligned.
- You can't give from depletion. You're most generous when you're well-nourished and deeply rooted.

Mantra: *I say no with love, so I can say yes with wholeness.*

Reconnect

Reconnection is the practice of returning to your center before extending to others. When you pause, ask, and act from a place of self-honoring, you create relationships rooted in clarity, not quiet resentment. You stop losing yourself and begin living as yourself.

- **Pause Before Committing**
  Ask: "Will this expand me or exhaust me?" Choose from awareness, not autopilot.

- **Practice Graceful Boundaries**
  Use language like: "I'd love to support you, but I need to honor my limits right now." Let your no be kind and clear.

- **Create Weekly Space Just for You**
  Block time for solitude, creativity, or rest. Protect it. Treat it as essential; because it is.

- **Offer Your Vitality, Not Your Leftovers**
  When you are rested, rooted, and restored, you give something far greater than effort; you give presence.

Affirmation: *I honor myself with every no. I protect my energy, nourish my joy, and give from overflow, not obligation.*

Final Thought: Let Self-Honoring Be Your Sacred Yes

You were not born to serve everyone but yourself.
You were born to live fully.
To love deeply.
To give generously, from overflow, not exhaustion.

When you honor your needs, you honor life itself.
When you speak your truth,
the world remembers its own.
Choosing yourself is not rejection; it is remembrance.
It is how love becomes whole.

Your "yes" is holy when it includes you.
Your peace is a prayer that blesses others.
Your boundaries are bridges, not walls.
Your rest is a revolution.

To honor yourself is to honor the divine within.
To live in truth is to live in grace.
And to choose yourself is to choose life.

This is Sovereign Living.

FAMILY ROLES TO INDIVIDUAL WHOLENESS

*"What you are to be,
you are now becoming."*
~ *Carl R. Rogers*

Every family has its cast of characters: the reliable one, the funny one, the caretaker, the rebel, the peacemaker. These roles form early, often unconsciously, shaped by dynamics, birth order, and need.

Sometimes they protect us.
Sometimes they define us.
But eventually, they can confine us.

The child who becomes "the strong one" may grow into an adult who doesn't know how to ask for help. The "achiever" may constantly strive for more, never feeling quite enough. The "fixer" may spend a lifetime tending to others' wounds while ignoring their own.

Family roles are survival strategies. But your healing begins when you recognize: you no longer need to survive your family. You get to grow beyond it.

My Story: From Obligation to Authenticity

I've worn many roles in my family.

The good daughter.
The dependable one.
The fixer.
The bridge.
The one who shows up no matter what.

These identities were both comforting and exhausting. They gave me a sense of purpose, but also an internal dialogue and unspoken rule: *Don't stray too far from who they need you to be.*

It wasn't until I reached my forties, through parenting, divorce, grief and rebuilding, that I truly began to ask:
What do I need?
Who am I without the script?

I remember one Thanksgiving, I chose not to host. I didn't offer to cook, coordinate, or clean up. Instead, I contributed a dish, brought wine and allowed myself to simply be. At first, the quiet in me felt foreign. The urge to jump up, manage, fix, and fill the space was internally loud. But I breathed through it.

That day I reclaimed a part of myself I had long suppressed: the woman who contributes with love, not obligation. The woman who enjoys presence over performance.

Since then, I've allowed more parts of myself to come forward: the playful woman, the writer, the mystic, the sacred space curator and the one who doesn't need to carry everything. And to my surprise, the world didn't fall apart when I let go of the old roles. It actually expanded.

Some relationships changed. Some expectations dissolved. And in their place, I found more truth, more connection and more peace.

From Role-Playing to Real Presence

Many of us were cast into roles early in life: the helper, the achiever, the peacemaker, the strong one, not as a choice, but as a way to belong. These roles, though protective in childhood, often become invisible cages in adulthood. This chapter invites you to step out of performance and into presence and to show up as your full self, not just the version that kept others comfortable.

Reflect

Reflection helps you recognize the roles you adopted in order to feel safe or loved. These patterns often follow us into adulthood, subtly influencing how we relate, achieve, and even self-evaluate. By seeing the role for what it was, a response to the environment, you gain the power to choose differently.

- What role did you play in your family of origin? Were you the fixer, the golden child, the invisible one, the caregiver?

- How has this role followed you into your work, friendships, or romantic relationships?

- Do you notice yourself shrinking back into that role when you're around family, even when it no longer fits?

Journaling Prompt: *What role have I outgrown and what is asking to emerge in its place?*

Reframe

Reframing allows you to see that your past role was a survival strategy, not a sentence. You are not betraying your family or your past by evolving. Presence doesn't ask you to abandon what was, but to stop performing it and start honoring who you are now.

- Your role was a response to the dynamics around you, not a definition of your identity.

- You are allowed to evolve beyond the version of you that made others comfortable.
- Letting go of the role isn't letting go of love, it's making space for authenticity, connection, and wholeness.

Mantra: *I don't need to perform to belong. My presence is enough.*

Reconnect

Reconnection is about showing up as your current self, especially in old spaces that try to pull you back into outdated scripts. It's about breaking the pattern gently, courageously, and with love, for yourself and for those who are ready to meet the real you.

- **Interrupt the Old Pattern**
  Choose one familiar situation where you tend to default to your old role. Pause. Breathe. Ask: "What does my present self want to say or do here?"

- **Give Others Permission to Evolve Too**
  When a family member shows up differently, with more openness, accountability, or softness, don't pull them back into their role either. Let everyone grow.

- **Create a New Tradition**
  Whether it's a shared ritual, a conversation, or a simple act of expression, begin something that reflects who you are today. Let it anchor your becoming.

- **Speak to Your Inner Child**
  Gently say:

- "Thank you for helping me belong."
- "You don't have to protect me anymore."
- "I'm free to grow now."

Affirmation: *I release the role. I reclaim my presence. I show up whole, not rehearsed.*

Final Thought: Step Out of the Role, Into Your Whole

You are not just the daughter, the mother,
the sister, the spouse.
You are a whole and radiant being.
Vast, alive, becoming.
The roles once kept you safe,
but they cannot hold your soul.

You were not born to shrink.
You were born to shine.
Family taught you devotion.
Now life teaches you expansion.

You are allowed to grow beyond
the version they remember.
You are allowed to become the woman
your spirit has been dreaming.
Wholeness is not rebellion.
It is a return.

Your rising becomes an invitation.
Your becoming gives others permission to breathe.
Let the old scripts fall away in gentleness and grace.
Step fully into your truth
and claim your life as your own.

This is Sovereign Living.

Part Three

MARRIAGE & PARTNERSHIP

CULTIVATING CONNECTION, TRUST, DEVOTION & SACRED INTIMACY

Marriage, in its Sovereign form, is not a contract but a conscious union, a daily choice to meet one another in truth, tenderness, and growth. It is where love evolves from instinct to intention, and partnership evolves into a sacred practice of presence and becoming.

In **Communication to Understanding**, words give way to empathy, where listening becomes love in motion and silence speaks of safety.

Through **Criticism to Trust & Respect**, judgment softens into compassion. Trust grows wild in the soil of kindness and honesty, rooting love in integrity.

Disconnection to Devotion & Partnership reminds you that commitment is not obligation but devotion, the steady rhythm of two Sovereign souls choosing to walk together.

In **Quality Time & Physical Touch to Intimacy**, presence becomes prayer. Touch becomes language. Connection becomes sacred.

And in **Conflict to Compassion and Forgiveness**, grace restores what ego has undone. Forgiveness frees both Hearts to begin again.

Marriage, as *Sovereign Living* teaches, is not the pursuit of perfection; it is the practice of presence. A meeting of two whole beings, each choosing again and again to love with awareness, humility, and awe.

COMMUNICATION TO UNDERSTANDING

"To love without knowing how to love wounds the person we love. To know how to love, we must learn to listen."

~ Thich Nhat Hanh

At the Heart of every relationship lies communication, both verbal and nonverbal. In marriage or partnership, it becomes the living current through which love, need, and identity flow. When children are present, communication extends beyond the couple; it becomes a model. They absorb how we express ourselves, how we listen, how we respond when tensions rise, and how we repair connection after rupture. Every word, gesture, and silence becomes part of their emotional education.

Communication is the foundation of partnership, but understanding is its true measure of success. Words alone cannot sustain intimacy; they must carry empathy, awareness, and presence. To communicate with understanding is to meet one another in truth and to listen for what is spoken and what is not, to hold curiosity for the needs beneath the words, and to remain open even when it feels easier to close. When we practice communication as a pathway to understanding, we move beyond the exchange of information into the creation of connection.

In Sovereign partnership, understanding transforms communication from reaction to relationship. It invites each person to become conscious of their inner world, their needs, fears, and desires, while honoring the same in the other. This is not about perfection, but presence. It is the daily practice of speaking with clarity, listening with care, and meeting one another with intention, so that both Hearts can feel seen and understood.

My Story: When the "We" Became "Us and Them"

My first husband and I were excellent communicators when it came to raising our children. We were aligned on nearly every aspect of family life, how to educate them, how to nourish them, how to set boundaries and create balance. Though I sometimes leaned toward being the stricter parent (and discipline was rare), we approached parenting as a united team. We shared the same values around time: family time, friend time, homework, sports, even vacations. This alignment created a home filled with harmony and laughter. The saying "you're only as happy as your unhappiest child" rang true for us, and we took pride in our children's happiness. They were deeply loved not only by us but by friends, extended family, and our wider community.

Where our communication faltered was in us, the couple at the center of it all. We excelled in the logistics of life, but rarely tended to the Heart of our partnership. In the early childbearing years, exhaustion made even the idea of a date night feel overwhelming. Outings usually included the children; they were the joyful constant in our world. As they grew and became more independent, I began to long for time alone with my husband, to reconnect, to celebrate, to dream. I suggested getaways for special occasions, from a nearby spa retreat to a trip to the Super Bowl. When those invitations were declined, I felt quietly rejected, but I also recognize now that I didn't yet have the language to express what those moments meant to me. I assumed he would understand that time together was my way of nurturing "us."

As the years went on, our social world revolved around other families. It was a wonderful, full life: laughter-filled dinners, children playing while adults shared stories late into the night. We functioned beautifully in that setting. We were a strong couple among others, well-liked and always included. But as our children approached high school, I began to envision a new chapter, a season just for us. I dreamed of selling our large home in Redding, moving closer to the beach and the train line in Fairfield, CT, for easier access to New York City. Eventually, when the children launched into their own lives, I imagined winters spent at our condo in Naples, FL, time for adventure, rest, and rediscovery as a couple.

One evening, we found ourselves talking about life after the children left home. It was a simple conversation, yet it changed everything. In that moment, I realized our visions were completely different. My dream included "us." His centered around the children.

I remember feeling confused and hurt. How could we both want the best for our family, yet hold such different ideas of what came next? I wanted to step into the next phase of life as partners rediscovering one another; he seemed to imagine continuing our roles as parents, still orbiting around our children's worlds. In hindsight, neither of us was wrong; we simply had different emotional anchors. I was ready to let go; he wasn't.

Instead of expressing my disappointment and inviting a deeper conversation, I withdrew. Conflict felt unbearable, and I told myself time would bring us closer again. Not long after, the sudden loss of my younger brother shifted everything. My energy turned entirely toward surviving the grief, and the space between us quietly grew wider.

The Space Between Words

At the Heart of every partnership is communication, not just the words exchanged, but the energy beneath them. Communication is the basic ingredient, yet its true success is understanding.

In marriage and partnership, communication becomes the current through which connection, trust, and intimacy flow. When understanding fades, communication fragments; words are spoken but not felt, and the space between two Hearts begins to widen.

This section invites you to move beyond talking to truly hearing, to see communication as the sacred bridge between self and other, where compassion begins and connection is restored.

Reflect

Reflection begins by observing your communication patterns with tenderness, not self-blame. Notice when you speak to be understood, and when you speak to be right. Notice how your partner communicates and what emotion or longing sits beneath their words.

- Identify where your communication patterns originate: family dynamics, past relationships, or unspoken fears.
- Recognize whether your needs come from love, fear, control, or longing.

- Understand how tone, timing, and body language can shift connection or distance.
- Observe how your partner expresses needs, through words, silence, or action.
- Remember: understanding your own needs is the first step toward truly hearing another's.

Journaling Prompt: *When do I feel most understood in my relationship, and what allows that to happen? What happens inside me when I feel unheard or dismissed?*

Reframe

Reframing is the art of shifting communication from defense to discovery. It's a choice to see communication as co-creation rather than competition. You are not trying to win; you are trying to understand.

- Shift the goal from being heard to creating understanding.
- Recognize that behind every criticism lies a veiled wish to be seen.
- Remember that both of you are learning to express love in different languages.
- Choose curiosity over assumption, softness over reaction.
- Understand that true listening invites empathy, not agreement.

Mantra: *I communicate to understand, not to defend. My words are bridges, not walls.*

Reconnect

Reconnection is the moment when understanding moves from thought into embodiment. Through shared presence, conversation, and touch, we restore what words alone cannot mend. The following practices invite rhythm, awareness, and emotional safety back into your relationship.

- **Venus Back Rolls**
  – Sit back-to-back with your partner, aligning spines and hips.
  – Inhale as you both lean gently against each other; exhale as you fold forward while your partner relaxes back.
  – Continue for several minutes, syncing breath and motion.

Focus: *Cultivate shared rhythm and quiet attunement, the unspoken harmony that arises when two bodies move as one.*

- **Seek Guided Conversation**
  – Schedule a session with a relationship or communications counselor trained in emotional intelligence.
  – The goal isn't to "fix" each other, but to learn tools for understanding underlying emotions, like fear, disappointment, or longing, that often hide beneath conflict.
  – A skilled guide can help you replace old patterns of reaction with new pathways of empathy and clarity.

Focus: *Build emotional fluency together. Learn to name what you feel and need without blame, creating a foundation of safety and trust.*

- **Listening Practice at Home**
  – Set aside 20 minutes each week for intentional listening. One partner speaks for five minutes while the other listens, with no interruptions, advice, or correction. Then switch roles.
  – Afterward, each person reflects back what they heard and what touched them most.

Focus: *Practice presence over problem-solving. Listening this way transforms ordinary conversation into emotional intimacy.*

Affirmation: *Through presence, listening, and understanding, we return to one another. Our words soften. Our Hearts align. Connection becomes our shared language and our living practice of love.*

Final Thought: From Words to Understanding

Communication bridges two inner worlds.
Love breathes through words, silence, and presence.
True connection asks for awareness.
It begins with knowing your needs.

Speak without armor.
Listen for the heart beneath words.
Understanding transforms distance into belonging.
It turns you and me into us.

Courage means seeing and being seen.
Pause before reacting.
Soften instead of defending.
Every criticism hides a wish for love.

Partnership thrives on presence, not perfection.
Daily choices shape connection.
Empathy over ego, connection over control.
Let communication lead you back to love.

This is Sovereign Living.

CRITICISM TO TRUST & RESPECT

"Behind every criticism is a veiled wish. We are very bad at knowing what we really want and probably even worse at communicating it."
~ Esther Perel

Criticism is often a form of self-protection disguised as truth-telling. When someone feels insecure, threatened, or unsure of their own worth, it can feel easier to attack than to admit vulnerability. Instead of saying, "I feel inadequate," or "I'm afraid I'm not enough," criticism often shows up as an insult, a jab, or a sweeping statement. Words rarely reveal the real wound underneath; they simply mirror the speaker's fear, not your truth.

Unlike a healthy complaint, which addresses a specific behavior, criticism attacks the person's character. It sends the message that who they are is the problem. Over time, these jabs chip away at the sense of safety and goodwill that every loving relationship depends on.

People often criticize because they don't feel emotionally safe enough to express softer feelings such as sadness, fear, longing, or need. Criticism gives the illusion of control; it keeps vulnerability at a distance. But what begins as protection soon becomes disconnection.

The impact is profound. Being criticized by the person you love feels like a rejection of your worth. It erodes trust, the belief that your partner sees the best in you, and diminishes respect, the sense that your voice and effort matter. As criticism becomes habitual, partners retreat into defensiveness or silence, each feeling misunderstood and alone.

Criticism doesn't create change; it creates distance. What heals instead is honesty spoken with tenderness, the courage to reveal the need beneath the complaint and invite understanding rather than attack.

My Story: The Words That Wounded Home

Early in our marriage, we lived in a small one-bedroom condo. I had hoped to wait to have children until we bought a home, but life, or perhaps God, had other plans. About a year after our wedding, I became pregnant, and we welcomed our first daughter into that tiny space. We made it work. Looking back, I understand that children arrive not on our schedule but in divine timing, exactly when we're ready, whether we believe it or not.

Because I was determined not to place her in daycare and we couldn't afford for me to stay home, my cousin offered to watch her. It was the perfect arrangement; she was already home with her own children and could use a little extra income. It felt like an answered prayer.

The only challenge was the distance. I drove from our condo in Stamford, CT, to my cousin's home in Port Chester, NY, and then back on the highway to my job near our condo. It became an exhausting hour-long round trip that often stretched even longer in traffic.

Still, I felt it was safer and more loving than leaving my daughter in a daycare setting. The blessing was that my cousin lived next door to our grandmother and her parents, so our firstborn was surrounded by generations of family, food, and affection. My father even delivered groceries and diapers when needed. Everyone played a part in caring for her.

When our daughter turned one, my parents decided to move from Port Chester to a quieter neighborhood nearby, in Rye Brook. They offered us their home temporarily, so we could save for our own house and spare our daughter those long commutes. We rented out our condo and paid my parents the rent we received. It was a gift: a bigger home, familiar neighbors, and the comfort of family close by. I was genuinely happy to be back in the place that had shaped me.

At the time, my husband and I worked for the same company. It had its perks: shared commutes, lunches together, mutual friends, and company volleyball games. One afternoon at lunch, a colleague asked how we liked living in Port Chester. I was ready to light up with gratitude, to talk about family support, safety, and relief from the daily grind.

But before I could answer, my husband jumped in with a laugh: "Oh my gosh, it's so loud there, with sirens, trains, and drunks breaking bottles by the gas station at night." He went on about the noise, the neighbors, and the above-ground pool sitting on a slab of concrete.

Everyone laughed and my Heart sank. While everything he said was true, it was my childhood home, the place I had loved and felt safe in. To me, it wasn't noise; it was life. I felt as though he hadn't just criticized a neighborhood; he'd criticized a piece of me, my parents, and the neighbors who had been nothing but kind to us.

I don't believe he meant to hurt me. He was being casual, maybe even trying to be funny. But his words cut deeply, leaving me embarrassed and unseen.

I didn't know how to express that pain, so instead I withdrew. I began to lose trust in his ability to protect what mattered to me, and I took on the role of doing everything myself to create stability and home.

Only years later did I realize how that one moment, and the pattern it revealed, quietly shifted the foundation of our relationship. What might have been a simple conversation became a turning point, teaching me how easily criticism can erode respect, and how silence, in response, can build walls where intimacy once lived.

From Reaction to Repair

When criticism enters a marriage, it slowly replaces curiosity with defensiveness and warmth with distance. Yet beneath every harsh word lies a quiet plea, a desire to be seen, valued, and understood. This section invites you to move from reaction to repair: to pause before defending, to listen before correcting, and to speak from need rather than blame. Through reflection, reframing, and reconnection, you can transform moments of tension into opportunities for trust, respect, and renewed intimacy.

Reflect

Criticism often begins where emotional safety ends. It's the armor we wear when our softer needs for love, respect, or appreciation feel unseen. Beneath every harsh word is a hidden longing: "See me." "Hear me." "Value me."

Reflection begins by noticing your own patterns with gentleness, not judgment. When do you criticize or feel criticized? What are you protecting beneath that reaction: fear, hurt, disappointment, or longing?

Understanding what lies under the criticism opens the door to compassion for both yourself and your partner.

- Recognize when criticism is actually a cover for unmet needs or unspoken fears
- Notice how you respond to criticism. Do you withdraw, defend, or counterattack?
- Identify moments when your tone or timing shuts connection instead of opening it.
- Become aware of how often you focus on what's wrong, instead of what's working.
- Remember: every complaint hides a hope and every harsh word, a wish to be understood.

Journaling Prompts: *When have I used criticism as protection rather than communication? What need or fear might have been underneath my words? When my partner criticizes me, what emotion rises first: shame, anger, sadness, or fear?*

Reframe

Reframing invites you to see criticism not as cruelty, but as confusion, a misdirected attempt to get needs met. Understanding this shifts the energy from defense to discovery.

Criticism says: "You're the problem."
Compassion says: "I have a need that isn't being met."

When you change your language from blame to clarity, your partner can finally hear you. Trust and respect grow when you speak from your own experience rather than attacking theirs.

- Shift from criticism: "You never help around the house" to complaint: "I feel overwhelmed when the kitchen stays messy. Can we divide tasks differently?"
- Remember that your partner's criticism is often their clumsy attempt to ask for connection.
- Take some responsibility for your part in the pattern.
- Replace defensiveness with curiosity: "What are they really trying to say?"
- Practice listening without interrupting; understanding is the antidote to criticism.

Mantra: *I choose understanding over accusation. I express my needs with clarity and care. Trust grows when both Hearts feel safe to be seen.*

Reconnect

Reconnection is how we rebuild safety after hurt. It's the conscious practice of softening walls, listening without defense, and offering appreciation where resentment once lived. Trust and respect are restored not in grand gestures, but in consistent, small acts of understanding.

- **Responding to Criticism Without Defending**
  When you feel attacked, your instinct may be to fight back or shut down. Instead, try moving toward your partner with gentle acknowledgment. Try one of these:
  – "That sounds really hard. Can we talk about what you need from me?"
  – "You're right, I have been distracted lately. I miss feeling close too."

– "It hurts to hear that, but I want to understand where it's coming from."

These responses don't mean you agree, they simply show that you value connection more than being right.

- **Complain, Don't Blame**
  A healthy complaint focuses on behavior, not character. Use these four parts to express your feelings clearly:
  – Take responsibility: "I realize I didn't communicate how tired I was."
  – Express how you feel: "I felt frustrated."
  – Be specific: "When the dishes weren't done last night."
  – State a positive need: "Could you help with cleanup tonight so we can both relax?"

- **Build a Culture of Trust and Respect**
  – Offer daily appreciation and name one thing your partner did well or that you admire.
  – Revisit your Love Map and ask questions that remind you who your partner is now, not just who they were.
  – Create moments of connection and share an end-of-day conversation, a walk, or a quiet meal without phones or distractions.
  – Apologize quickly, forgive gently because every repair builds a layer of trust.
  – Admire out loud because respect grows when we remember to say, "I'm proud of you," or "I love the way you handled that."

Affirmation: *I replace judgment with understanding, criticism with curiosity, and blame with truth spoken in love. In this, trust and respect are reborn, quietly, steadily, and strong.*

Final Thought: Where Trust Begins Again

Trust is not built in grand gestures,
but in the quiet moments of choosing to stay.
It begins where presence meets honesty,
where curiosity softens the edges of fear.

Each time you listen instead of defend,
a bridge is rebuilt, plank by plank.
Compassion takes the place of control,
and love remembers how to breathe.

Criticism divides; understanding unites.
Respect grows in the soil of safety.
When two Hearts feel seen and human,
they begin again, not perfectly, but truly.

Let every word be a seed of repair.
Let every silence hold grace, not distance.
This is how love matures, through awareness,
not avoidance.

This is Sovereign Living.

DISCONNECTION TO DEVOTION & PARTNERSHIP

"Love is not two people gazing at each other, but two people looking outward together in the same direction."
~ Antoine de Saint-Exupéry

Disconnection is not always the absence of love. Sometimes, it's love longing for renewal. In every long-term partnership, there are seasons when closeness fades under the weight of responsibilities, routines, and unspoken hurts. What was once effortless connection can quietly become parallel living.

Devotion is how we return, through choice, presence, and care. It is the sacred act of showing up again and again, even when it would be easier to turn away. Partnership rooted in devotion is not built on perfection, but on the daily decision to repair rather than retreat, to prioritize "we" over "me."

In this chapter, we explore how couples can transform disconnection into deeper partnership, not by avoiding conflict or difference, but by honoring love as a living practice. Devotion is born from awareness, forgiveness, and shared purpose. It is the mature form of love that grows not because life is easy, but because both Hearts keep saying yes to growth, even through the hard days.

My Story: A Steady Fire

There is one marriage I have admired for over forty years. My cousin Connie and her husband Jeff's relationship has never been all rainbows and perfection, but rather a living portrait of deep devotion, the kind that endures, evolves, and refuses to give up. After all these years, they still cannot imagine life without one another.

Their love story began at fourteen. We were in Catholic school, and Jeff attended the local public school. Each afternoon he'd pass by, calling out her name with a grin, waiting out front just to catch a glimpse of her. Sometimes he'd sneak over late at night to whisper through her bedroom window, and during sleepovers, I'd help cover for her, as cousins do. They dated all through high school until a breakup their senior year led them to different prom dates. Everyone around them seemed more heartbroken than they were.

A few years later, while in college, they reconnected, realizing that time and distance hadn't dimmed their love. At just twenty-three, they married, and soon after, began their family. Three beautiful children filled their home, and Connie's dream of being a stay-at-home mother became reality because Jeff worked tirelessly to make it possible. It wasn't always easy, but together, they built a life defined by teamwork and trust.

They took modest vacations, cheered at every game, and put all three children through college, even hosting two gorgeous weddings. They have sacrificed much for their family, but never at the expense of each other. Through it all, they protected their time as a couple. Date nights were non-negotiable. One of their daughters once laughed, "I felt bad asking Mommy and Daddy to babysit on their date night!" To make it up to them, she bought a gift card to their favorite restaurant and booked a reservation herself.

Even through health scares, career stress, and the challenges of aging parents, Connie and Jeff have remained like two pillars, strong, steady, and side by side. They have had their fiery arguments, yes, but never their undoing. At the end of every storm, they return to one another with softness and humor.

Jeff has always been the protector and provider, not out of duty, but devotion. Connie, in turn, has been the Heart of harmony, grounding their home with warmth and grace. Together, they are proof that love is not about avoiding disconnection, but learning how to find your way back, again and again.

Theirs is a Sovereign partnership, imperfect, passionate, and unbreakable.

The Journey Back to "We"

Disconnection often begins quietly. It's not always born from conflict, but from slow drift, the way daily routines, unspoken hurts, or unmet needs begin to replace laughter and closeness. Love becomes management. Partnership turns into coexistence. But beneath the distance, devotion still lives, waiting to be remembered.

This is the journey from distance to a partnership rooted in devotion, the movement from isolation toward intimacy, from duty toward shared joy, from surviving together to truly living together.

Reflect

Reflection begins by noticing the spaces where connection has thinned. Not with blame, but with curiosity. Where have you become partners in logistics rather than lovers in life? What moments of tenderness have been replaced by silence or habit?

- Recognize the subtle ways disconnection shows up, emotional absence, irritability, or indifference.
- Acknowledge what once connected you, shared laughter, curiosity, physical closeness, and where it was lost.
- Identify how you each reach for one another when things feel distant.
- Remember that devotion is not a feeling you lose, but a practice you return to.

Journaling Prompts: *Where have I stopped reaching for my partner? What gestures, words, or habits once made us feel close? What does devotion look like to me now and how am I nurturing it?*

Reframe

Reframing begins with seeing disconnection not as failure, but as a signal, an invitation back to awareness. Every relationship cycles between closeness and distance. Devotion is not about avoiding the ebb; it's about learning to meet the tide with presence.

- Shift from "We're growing apart" to "We're being asked to grow differently."
- Understand that partnership isn't a constant state of harmony; it's a dance of returning.
- See time apart or silence not as rejection, but as a pause inviting renewal.
- Recommit to small gestures that say, "I still choose us."

Mantra: *I honor the seasons of love. I meet distance with curiosity, not fear. Devotion is my daily return to the Heart of "we."*

Reconnect

Reconnection is how devotion becomes embodied, not through grand gestures, but through small, sacred acts of presence. It's the choice to make time, to touch, to look into each other's eyes and remember why you began.

- **Carve Out Sacred Time**
  Schedule time together that is non-negotiable. This is not a "date night," but a sacred pause, a weekly ritual of devotion. Put away devices, slow your breath, and simply be in one another's presence.

- **Return to Touch**
  Physical touch is a language of reassurance. A hand on the back, an embrace in the kitchen, fingers brushing across the table, small, intentional contact rekindles trust and safety.

- **Devotion as Motion**
  Let intimacy be an expression of reverence, not performance. When you touch your partner, do it with mindfulness, as if saying, "I see you, I cherish you." Whether in lovemaking or gentle affection, let touch be prayer, not proof.

- **The Evening Practice**
  Before bed, spend five minutes in shared gratitude. Speak one truth you appreciated about the other that day. End with a touch, a hand over the Heart, a soft kiss, or a silent thank you. These moments stitch connection back into daily life.

- **Seek Support When Needed**
  If old wounds or patterns of distance persist, seek the guidance of a couples therapist or communication coach. Sometimes devotion begins with learning new tools to be heard and to hear.

Affirmation: *We return to one another through presence. We choose time over distraction, tenderness over distance.*

Final Thought: Love Is the Daily Return

Love doesn't disappear; it drifts, then waits.
It lingers in the pause,
the quiet ache, the tender space between.
Devotion is how we find our way back.

Love is not the absence of distance,
but the courage to bridge it.
To reach across silence.
To whisper, "I'm still here."

The smallest gestures become the loudest prayers.
Partnership is not a promise to never wander,
but a vow to always return.
To choose presence over pride,
softness over silence,
hands over words.

Because love is motion, a rhythm,
a return, a remembering.
It is not perfection, but a practice,
and the daily choice to stay.

This is Sovereign Living.

QUALITY TIME & PHYSICAL TOUCH TO INTIMACY

"The goal is to speak the language of your partner's love, not your own. When you speak their language, they feel loved and appreciated."

~ Dr. Gary Chapman

Intimacy is not just about physical closeness, it's about emotional fluency. It's learning to love your partner in the language that makes them feel most alive, most safe, and most seen.

If you've ever read *The 5 Love Languages: The Secret to Love That Lasts* by Dr. Gary Chapman, you know that love is expressed and received in unique ways. What makes you feel loved, whether it's through words, time, touch, gifts, or service, may not be what your partner needs to feel the same.

The five love languages are described as:

- Acts of Service
- Receiving Gifts
- Quality Time
- Words of Affirmation
- Physical Touch

You can discover your own and your partner's at LoveLanguage.com, through a free self-assessment.

In this chapter, we'll focus on two languages, **Quality Time** and **Physical Touch**, because when they align, they create the foundation for intimacy. Intimacy is not just sex; it's safety, playfulness, and presence. It's the experience of being known and loved as your full self.

According to multiple national surveys, **Quality Time** is the most common primary love language (about 40% of people), followed by **Physical Touch** (about 22%). Together, these two represent nearly two-thirds of how most men and women experience love, confirming that connection is not built on words alone, but on time and tenderness.

My Story: When Love Needed a New Language

One crisp fall morning, I walked with my dear friend along the shoreline, the ocean quiet and steady beside us. I asked how her new relationship was going. To anyone observing them, they seemed perfectly matched, both creative spirits with a shared love of architecture, cooking, and hosting dinner parties that felt like celebrations of art and friendship.

I had watched them together before, him gently correcting her on how to roll rice paper for an appetizer, her laughing and welcoming the advice. In another lifetime, she might have bristled, but now there was an ease between them. Their smiles and the brief touches as they passed each other in the kitchen created a picture of harmony.

As we walked, her eyes softened as she described his thoughtful gestures fixing things around the house, sending small gifts when she admired something in his kitchen, and anticipating her needs before she even spoke. "His nervous system regulates mine," she said. I knew exactly what she meant. It is that rare feeling when being near someone calms you, where safety and affection coexist.

But then came the pause. The "but."

She hesitated before saying, "I'm yearning for something deeper, more passion, more playfulness. We have quality time and affection, but the spark, the intensity of intimacy, feels missing. I don't know how to say that without making him feel like he's not enough."

I could feel her conflict with how to honor what was good without betraying what *wasn't*.

I suggested she first set the stage with intention, to let him know she wanted to have a Heart-centered conversation soon so it wouldn't feel like an ambush. Then, when they were next together, to go for a walk, as movement softens tension and nature holds space for truth.

I suggested to her: *Begin with love.* Tell him what you cherish about him. What feels easy. What you adore. Only then share the desire.

Explain to him that physical touch and quality time mean so much to you. Let him know you would love to explore an even deeper connection between the two of you, more adventure, more play. Let him know that you love how gentle he is, and sometimes you crave a little more intensity. Ask if he would be open to that, maybe every other time you're intimate?"

When she later told me how the conversation went, she smiled. Her partner had laughed with tenderness and said, "Of course I could be more intense for you." There was no rejection, only understanding, because she had spoken from Sovereignty, not from lack.

That's the Heart of **Sovereign Living**: expressing your needs without fear, trusting that honesty, offered with love, deepens connection rather than destroys it.

From Presence to Intimacy

Intimacy is not found in grand gestures; it's created in moments of shared presence. It's the way you listen, the warmth of a hand on your back, the laughter that returns you to each other after distance. In **Sovereign Living**, intimacy begins when two people choose to show up fully, mind, body, and soul, and meet one another with openness instead of performance.

This section invites you to explore how time, touch, and intention transform ordinary connection into something sacred and sustaining.

Reflect

True intimacy starts with awareness, not of your partner, but of yourself. Before you can receive or give touch, you must first understand what you need to feel safe, desired, and emotionally present.

- Notice what intimacy means to you. Is it closeness, vulnerability, play, or tenderness?
- Explore when you feel most connected: quiet conversation, shared laughter, gentle touch, or passionate exchange.
- Observe what pulls you away from intimacy. Is it fatigue, resentment, distraction, or fear of rejection.
- Ask yourself: "Do I allow myself to be touched emotionally before physically?"

Journaling Prompts: *What does "being truly intimate" mean to me? When do I feel most open to giving and receiving love? How do I show my partner that I desire them, not just love them?*

Reframe

Intimacy is not a duty; it's an energy exchange and a conversation without words. When we equate physical touch with obligation or pressure, it disconnects us from our bodies and each other. Reframing intimacy means understanding it as a form of sacred communication and a place where love, safety, and desire coexist.

- See physical connection as an invitation, not a demand.
- Communicate your desires with curiosity instead of criticism.
- Express needs as truth, not as test: "I miss feeling close to you" instead of "You never touch me anymore."
- Recognize that your partner may speak a different "love dialect" and your openness invites theirs.

Mantra: *My body is a vessel of love. I give and receive with presence, not performance.*

Reconnect

Reconnection turns reflection into action: the embodied expression of trust and love. It's where presence becomes passion. These practices invite you to slow down, to feel, and to build a deeper rhythm of intimacy.

- **Tantric Gazing, The Eyes as the First Touch**
  Sit facing one another, knees touching if comfortable. Light a candle between you. Breathe together: slow, steady, and unforced. Gaze softly into each other's eyes for 2–3 minutes. Notice what arises, awkwardness, emotion, warmth, and simply stay.

This is the essence of tantra: seeing and being seen without judgment. Build energetic connection before physical contact.

- **Setting the Room for Romance**
  – Transform your space into a sanctuary of intimacy. Dim the lights, light candles, use essential oils like rose or sandalwood. Choose music that soothes the senses, soft textures, and perhaps lingerie that makes you feel confident and alive, not for performance, but embodiment.
  – Signal to your body and spirit that it is safe to open, receive, and give.

- **The Touch of Presence**
  – Using natural oils, take turns offering a slow, intentional body massage, not for arousal alone, but for relaxation and reconnection. Begin with the intention, "I'm here to honor you." Breathe deeply and stay mindful of each touch.
  – Touch as a sacred exchange, giving without agenda, receiving without guilt.

- **Quality Time Ritual**
  – Create a weekly ritual that prioritizes uninterrupted time, an evening walk, dinner without phones, or simply lying together in silence. The body relaxes when time slows.
  – Build safety and consistency, the soil where passion naturally grows.

Affirmation: *Through presence, touch, and time, we remember that intimacy is not what we do and it is how we become. In this becoming, love turns from habit to holiness.*

Final Thought: The Sacred Language of Connection

Intimacy lives in quiet rhythm,
a glance,
a breath,
a touch that whispers, *I'm here.*

Quality time is devotion.
Physical touch is prayer.
Together, they form the sacred language of love,
not spoken, but felt.

When we honor both, we transcend habit into holiness.
Connection deepens. Awareness expands.
Desire softens into safety.
Stillness burns with quiet fire.

To love this way is to worship the present moment,
to see and be seen without defense or demand,
to rest in the truth that presence is passion.

This is Sovereign Living.

CONFLICT TO COMPASSION & FORGIVENESS

> *"A happy marriage is not the absence of conflict, but the presence of forgiveness."*
> *~ Dr. Robert Anthony*

Conflict is not the enemy of love; it is often the moment love reveals where it needs to grow. In every enduring relationship, there are seasons when tension, misunderstanding, or disappointment arise, testing the strength of the bond. Conflict exposes the places where our wounds meet, where expectations collide, and where silence can become a form of protection.

Compassion is how we begin to soften those sharp edges. It asks us to look beneath the argument and see the ache beneath the words, to respond not from ego but from empathy. Forgiveness is the bridge that follows. It is not the erasure of pain, but the conscious decision to release resentment and choose peace over pride.

In this chapter, we explore how couples can transform conflict into a path of deeper intimacy. Through compassion, accountability, and forgiveness, we learn that harmony is not found in the absence of disagreement, but in the presence of grace. True partnership thrives when both Hearts are willing to repair rather than retreat, to meet one another, again and again, in understanding.

My Story: Forty Years of Devotion

Some love stories are defined not by grand gestures, but by quiet endurance, the daily act of choosing grace when pride would be easier. Celebrity couple Denzel and Pauletta Washington's forty-year marriage is one such story: a living testament to devotion shaped by faith, humor, and forgiveness.

Their journey began in humility, long before fame or fortune. They met on the set of *Wilma* in the late 1970s, and while their connection was instant, Pauletta turned down Denzel's first two marriage proposals before finally saying yes. Those early refusals were not rejections; they were reflections of discernment, a pause that deepened understanding. Even then, they were practicing what would become the foundation of their union: patience and respect.

When they married in 1983, their beginnings were modest. There's a now-famous story of Denzel running out of money on their first date and Pauletta paying for the taxi. That moment, simple, human, and unromantic, became symbolic of their partnership. They would spend the next four decades doing what that small act embodied: sharing burdens, lifting one another, and meeting life's challenges as a team.

As Denzel's career ascended, Pauletta set aside her own ambitions to nurture their family and create a home anchored in love and stability. She became the quiet force behind his success, the grounding presence in the swirl of fame. He, in turn, never failed to acknowledge her sacrifices, once saying, "You can buy a house, but that doesn't make it a home. My wife made our house a home."

Their marriage, like all long partnerships, has known its tests: public scrutiny, demanding careers, and the inevitable frictions of time. Yet they've met those challenges with unwavering faith and humor. Pauletta has spoken about the power of "staying in forgiveness mode," an acknowledgment that love is not sustained by perfection but by mercy, the daily willingness to release resentment and begin again.

In 1995, they renewed their vows in South Africa in a ceremony officiated by Archbishop Desmond Tutu; it was a symbolic recommitment to both faith and partnership. It wasn't a spectacle; it was sacred renewal. That act, like so many others, reflected a truth at the Heart of enduring love: forgiveness is not forgetting, but remembering with compassion.

After forty years together, Denzel still refers to Pauletta as his rock. When asked the secret to their longevity, he laughs, "I do what I'm told. I keep my mouth shut." Beneath the humor lies a deeper wisdom: the understanding that peace in partnership comes not from control but from surrender, humility, and respect.

Their story reminds us that conflict is inevitable, but disconnection is optional. They have proven that compassion and forgiveness are not moments but a rhythm, a practice of softening again and again in the face of human imperfection. Through faith, devotion, and laughter, they show what it means to evolve together rather than apart.

The Space Between Hurt and Healing

Conflict doesn't end love; it tests its depth. Every relationship encounters moments of friction where words sting and distance grows. Yet beneath every disagreement lies a hidden longing: to be seen, heard, and understood. Compassion invites us to pause before reacting, to breathe before speaking, and to look beneath the anger to the tenderness underneath.

When we meet conflict with empathy instead of ego, something sacred happens; pain softens, and understanding begins to bloom. Forgiveness then becomes the bridge back to connection. It is not forgetting or excusing, but releasing the need to be right so love can rise again. In forgiveness, we remember that both Hearts are learning, both are human, and both are worthy of grace.

Reflect

Every relationship carries moments of misunderstanding, hurt, or disappointment. Reflection invites you to pause before reaction, to look inward, not for blame, but for awareness. Conflict often reveals what is unspoken: unmet needs, unhealed wounds, or fears of disconnection. When you reflect with compassion, you begin to understand that conflict is not a failure, but an invitation to grow.

- Recognize your own triggers and emotional patterns during conflict.
- Ask yourself what you're truly feeling beneath anger: fear, sadness, or longing.
- Notice how your partner may express hurt differently than you do.
- Remember that both of you want the same thing at the core: to feel loved, heard, and valued.

- Understand that forgiveness begins with empathy, seeing your partner's humanity before defending your own.

Journaling Prompts: *What am I really needing when I feel angry or defensive? When have I felt misunderstood, and how did I respond? What would it look like to extend compassion to both myself and my partner in moments of tension?*

Reframe

Reframing allows you to shift from being right to being real. It transforms conflict from a battlefield into sacred ground for healing. When you reframe a disagreement, you no longer see your partner as the opponent, but as someone struggling, just like you, to be understood.

- Replace judgment with curiosity: "Help me understand what you're feeling."
- Speak in ways that calm rather than inflame: "I hear that you felt hurt when I said that."
- Remember that forgiveness doesn't condone harm; it releases the need to punish.
- Acknowledge your part in the misunderstanding without self-blame.
- Shift from "you always" to "I notice" or "I feel," which invites dialogue rather than defense.

Mantra: *I choose peace over pride. I choose understanding over control. I am willing to see through eyes of compassion.*

Reconnect

Reconnection is where healing becomes action; where compassion is practiced, not just felt. It is the soft return to each other after the storm, the quiet rebuilding of trust through words and gestures of care.

- **Write a Letter of Forgiveness**
  Begin not with your own feelings, but with your partner's. Acknowledge their hurt first: "I understand how my words made you feel unseen." Speak to their experience before explaining your own. This simple act opens the Heart and lowers defenses.

- **Use Soft Starts**
  Begin difficult conversations with warmth and humility. Instead of, "You never listen," try, "I know we've both been tired lately. Can we talk about how to make this easier for both of us?"

- **Seek Counsel**
  When patterns repeat or emotions run deep, consider seeking help from a communication or relationship counselor who can guide you toward understanding the emotions beneath the conflict.

- **Touch and Presence**
  After resolution, restore closeness through small, sacred gestures: holding hands, sitting in silence, gentle touch. Physical connection can speak what words cannot.

- **Create Rituals of Repair**
  End difficult days with an act of renewal, a walk, prayer, shared laughter, or gratitude before sleep.

Affirmation: *Forgiveness is my bridge from hurt to healing. Through compassion, love returns and endures.*

Final Thought: The Quiet Work of the Heart

Conflict is inevitable; disconnection is optional.
It begins with a spark of misunderstanding,
but it can end in the stillness of compassion.

When we pause before defending,
when we listen instead of react,
we open the doorway for grace to enter.

Forgiveness is not weakness; it is wisdom.
It says, I value peace more than pride.
It turns hurt into humility,
and judgment into understanding.

Love matures here,
in the gentle courage to repair,
to choose tenderness when anger tempts,
to hold the Heart of another as sacred as your own.

Let hurt soften.
Let pride loosen.
Let compassion lead.
Let love return.

This is Sovereign Living.

Part Four

DIVORCE
HEALING THROUGH ACCOUNTABILITY, FORGIVENESS & LOVE

Divorce is not the end of love; it is the transformation of it. It is the journey from unconscious reaction to conscious release, from breaking apart to breaking open. It is the tender unfolding of wisdom that pain leaves behind, the moment the Heart begins to see endings as openings.

In **Unconscious to Conscious Uncoupling**, you awaken from old patterns of attachment to walk the path of awareness, compassion, and emotional maturity. **Revenge to Peaceful Resolution** reminds you that closure is not won through conflict, but through grace, the quiet strength of choosing peace over punishment and presence over pride.

Through **Blame to Accountability**, you step into radical self-honesty, seeing not just what happened to you, but what is asking to be healed within you. **Resentment to Radical Forgiveness** becomes the alchemy that frees your Heart, transforming pain into wisdom and bitterness into blessing. And in **Rejection to Acceptance**, you remember that nothing real can ever be lost; it can only be transformed, refined, and returned to love in a higher form.

This passage is an invitation to reimagine separation as sacred evolution, a season of truth, tenderness, and release. Each chapter guides you home to yourself, where healing becomes not about letting go of another, but about finally returning in wholeness to you, stronger, softer, and infinitely more aware.

UNCONSCIOUS TO CONSCIOUS UNCOUPLING

"Your breakup doesn't need to ruin your life, damage your kids, or define your future."
~ Katherine Woodward Thomas

When a marriage ends, most of us long for an amicable separation, a peaceful transition into two new lives built on respect rather than resentment. But as Katherine Woodward Thomas wisely reminds us, "Hurt people often hurt people." Without awareness, heartbreak can easily turn hostile.

The concept of *"Conscious Uncoupling"*, the respectful, compassionate ending of a relationship, was introduced by Katherine and later brought into the mainstream at the onset of the marital separation between Gwyneth Paltrow and Chris Martin. At its Heart, it's a revolutionary idea: two people choosing to part not as adversaries, but as conscious partners, committed to integrity, especially when children are involved.

My Story: Grace Beyond the Legal Lines

Looking back, my divorce was conscious in its decision, but largely unconscious in its execution.

There was no manual, no guidebook. Only a sincere intention to minimize harm, and the inevitable human missteps along the way.

I wanted mediation. A clean, 50/50 split of time with the children and our assets. It felt fair.

But when the suggestion to sell the marital home during mediation surfaced, a way to keep both parents nearby and co-parent effectively, something shifted. My soon to be former husband hired an aggressive attorney, and the tone changed. Mediation gave way to litigation.

In response, I hired a team of three female attorneys known for their fairness and balanced approach. Together, we stood by the original intention: equity, respect, and the best interest of our children. But paper agreements can't govern Hearts.

Despite our written 50/50 parenting plan, two of my children struggled to follow it. They were trying to make sense of a difficult transition, one that reshaped their understanding of family and challenged their sense of stability. They had been told about an emotional connection I formed outside the marriage, and without the full context, it was hard for them to understand what was true and what it meant for our family. Their distance was painful, but it reflected their inner overwhelm, not a lack of love.

During this time, someone who had been in my professional world for quite a while became a steady source of support. He offered encouragement, perspective, and kindness as I navigated the grief of losing my brother while balancing both my work and my role as a mother. Only after my marital separation did that consistent presence evolve into a dating relationship.

My children did not have the full picture, and the information they received shaped their understanding in ways that were difficult for each of us. I understood they were responding to protect their sense of safety and make sense of an adult situation. They were young, holding more emotion than they knew how to name, and simply doing their best to find steadiness in a season that felt confusing and uncertain.

Their distance was never about a lack of love. It was an attempt to create clarity in a moment when nothing felt clear. And even in the hardest moments, my love for them remained constant, spacious, and unwavering.

Ending with Grace, Parenting with Purpose

Divorce or separation does not have to be the collapse of everything; it can be the conscious transformation of what no longer serves into something wiser, clearer, and more aligned. Consciously Uncoupling is not about erasing pain, but about choosing dignity over destruction. And conscious parenting through and beyond separation becomes the legacy you leave, one built not on blame, but on presence, respect, and love.

Reflect

Reflection invites you to gently explore the emotional and societal narratives surrounding your separation. Beyond the logistics and legalities, there's often unspoken grief; not just for the relationship, but for the identity and vision that once accompanied it. Before healing can deepen, these quiet truths must be named.

- Have you allowed yourself to grieve the end of the relationship *and* the dream it once held?
- Where in your story did you respond from unresolved pain, fear, or pride rather than grounded clarity?

- What cultural or familial messages around failure, divorce, or separation are still shaping how you view yourself today?

Journaling Prompt: *What part of my past do I need to grieve or forgive so I can step forward with clarity and peace?*

Reframe

Reframing transforms the story of loss into one of evolution. Divorce is not a failure; it's a shift in form. Choosing to uncouple with intention honors what was, while making space for what can still be, especially in how you parent. When the foundation shifts, your values, not your resentments, must lead.

- Divorce is a transition and it can be navigated with grace, growth, and respect.
- Conscious Uncoupling doesn't remove the pain, but it centers purpose and intention over reaction.
- Co-parenting is not the end of your partnership; it's the final, and possibly most meaningful, act of your shared responsibility.

Mantra: *This ending is not my failure; it is my evolution, and I choose to walk it with love and clarity.*

Reconnect

Reconnection is about choosing presence over pride, especially when children are involved. Healing doesn't mean recreating the past, but redefining what family, respect, and love look like now. When you anchor your actions in what's best for the next generation, you write a story of strength, not just for them, but for yourself.

- **Center the Children's Well-being**
  Let every major decision reflect their needs, not your pain or desire to punish. Legacy matters more than control.

- **Reflect and Integrate Your Growth**
  Journal what the relationship taught you about love, truth, boundaries, identity, and resilience. Let your lessons lead your next chapter.

- **Seek and Accept Support**
  Work with a therapist, coach, or spiritual guide. This path is heavy alone, lighter when walked in community.

- **Redefine "Family" with Intention**
  Let go of the idealized past. Explore new ways to embody love, inclusion, and healing. Family is not form; it's how we choose to show up.

Affirmation: *I release the past with gratitude, lead my future with intention, and parent with presence, compassion, and clarity.*

Final Thought: Choose Peace Over Punishment

Divorce is not the end of love,
it's the evolution of it.
It's the moment you stop fighting to be right
and start choosing to be free.

You don't need to destroy what once was
to honor what still can be.

You can close a chapter with grace,
and begin again with intention.

Conscious Uncoupling isn't breaking apart;
it's breaking open.
Open to healing.
Open to growth.
Open to rewriting what family means from here.

Peace is the legacy.
Love, redefined, is the reward.

This is Sovereign Living.

REVENGE TO PEACEFUL RESOLUTION

*"Weak people revenge.
Strong people forgive.
Intelligent people ignore."*
~ Albert Einstein

When conflict arises, in love, family, or business, the most liberating choice we can make is to pursue peace over punishment.

Revenge may feel momentarily satisfying, but it anchors us in the very pain we're trying to escape. It replays the wound and binds our energy to an old story. The longer we stay in that story, the more life we give to the hurt, and the harder it becomes to move on.

Peaceful resolution doesn't always mean reconciliation. It means reclaiming your energy and walking away with grace, for yourself, and for the collective healing of all involved.

My Story: Choosing Grace, Not Retaliation

The breakdown of my marriage was painful, but it didn't need to become a battlefield.

From the beginning, I wanted fairness. I believed in mediation, shared parenting, and equal division of time and assets. I had no desire to punish or deplete, only to restructure our lives in a way that honored everyone involved, especially our children.

But as the legal process unfolded, patterns such as control, fear and ego emerged. What began as a shared vision slowly shifted into a struggle, one I didn't initiate, but one I had to now navigate with strength and restraint.

I saw clearly how quickly divorce could become a war, not because of one big betrayal, but because of smaller, quieter fractures:

- A failure to communicate clearly.
- A misalignment of expectations.
- A breakdown of respect.

And when children are involved, the stakes are higher. I watched as the emotional impact reached them in ways I couldn't always protect. Parental sparation isn't always overt. Sometimes it's a subtle silence, a story or a shift in loyalty that's too mature for their years. It's painful, but I chose not to retaliate. I chose peace.

Was I perfect in the process? No. But I made a conscious decision: I would not fuel conflict. I would not weaponize pain or the children. I would walk forward with integrity, even when the path felt lonely.

And that choice set me free.

How to Remain Strong Without Going to War

Strength is not always about standing your ground; sometimes, it's about laying down the battle altogether. When we confuse peace with weakness, we stay stuck in cycles of retaliation and emotional depletion. But true Sovereignty is found in choosing clarity over chaos, and release over revenge. This chapter is an invitation to redefine strength, not as control over others, but as mastery over yourself.

Reflect

Reflection invites you to examine the emotional residue of conflict. Where are you still holding on to pain, blame, or the need to be right? Sometimes the weight of unresolved tension becomes heavier than the original wound. Let yourself ask what part of the story you're still carrying, and what it might look like to finally put it down.

- Have you held onto anger or resentment in a way that's delayed your healing or growth?
- Are you seeking affirmation or approval from others to justify your pain or position, including from your children?
- What specific moment or comment from the conflict do you revisit often, and what are you hoping it will give you?

Journaling Prompt: *What part of this story am I ready to release, not for them, but for me?*

Reframe

Reframing helps you understand that peace is not passivity; it's power. Releasing the need to retaliate or "win" doesn't mean you were wrong. It means you've decided to protect your energy, your healing, and your future. Justice isn't found in retribution; it's found in restoring your inner equilibrium.

- Revenge doesn't restore balance; it extends pain.
- You don't need closure in the form of an apology to choose freedom.

- Peace is not the absence of power; it's the highest form of it.

Mantra: *I protect my peace not by fighting harder, but by letting go with intention and grace.*

Reconnect

Reconnection invites you to channel your energy away from proving your pain and into reclaiming your presence. Let go of the need to be understood by those who cannot meet you there. Instead, ground yourself in self-honoring practices that restore your clarity, emotional Sovereignty, and strength.

- **Write to Release**
  Write a letter to express everything you wish had done differently. You don't have to send it, just let the truth move through you and out of you.

- **Reclaim Your Attention**
  Where your attention goes, your energy flows. Redirect your focus to what restores your health, your joy, and your future.

- **Create New Agreements with Yourself**
  Write and repeat:
  – "I choose clarity over chaos"
  – "I choose release over retaliation."
  – "I choose peace over proving a point."

Affirmation: *My strength is my softness, my silence, and my Sovereignty. I release the need to win, and I rise in peace.*

Final Thought: Choose Peace Even When You Have the Power to Hurt

You don't need revenge to be right.
You don't need validation to be free.
You don't need to win a war that wounds your soul.

Strength is restraint.
Power is peace.
Grace is the language of the Sovereign Heart.

Walk away without the last word,
and let silence speak your wisdom.
Let your calm be your statement.
Let your integrity be your legacy.

Choose clarity over chaos.
Choose presence over pride.
Choose love, even when it's no longer returned.

This is how you rise.
This is how you lead.

This is Sovereign Living.

BLAME TO ACCOUNTABILITY

> *"When we fail to set boundaries and hold people accountable, we feel used and mistreated. This is why we sometimes attack who they are, which is far more hurtful than addressing a behavior or a choice."*
>
> ~ Brené Brown

Blame gives us something to hold onto when our Hearts feel fractured. It lets us point a finger, assign responsibility, and seek emotional refuge in a story where we are the one wronged. But that story, if we stay in it too long, becomes a cage.

True healing comes not from assigning blame, but from owning our part. This is accountability. And accountability is the most radical form of self-respect.

We cannot control every event in our lives. But we can control our responses. We can name the silent expectations we never voiced. We can take responsibility for the boundaries we failed to set, the truths we withheld, and the times we didn't honor our own inner knowing.

My Story: Liberation Through Honest Reflection

When my marriage ended, I wanted to understand *why*. I wanted to know where things went wrong, not just to assign fault, but to free myself from repeating the same patterns.

In reflection, I discovered something tender and humbling: I had been projecting a silent, inherited expectation, one shaped by the men I grew up around. My father, grandfather, and uncles were traditional providers. They offered safety and financial security. They carried burdens silently and led without hesitation.

Unconsciously, I assumed my husband would step into that same model. But we had never spoken about it. There was no mutual agreement, no aligned vision. And when life didn't mirror my inherited blueprint, when I had to return to work just six weeks postpartum, I felt a quiet grief that eventually hardened into resentment.

But the truth is: my former husband never failed me. He never promised to be the only provider. He did promise to be a fully present and engaged dad, and he kept that promise.

The unmet expectation was mine. And the liberation came when I saw that clearly, without shame, without blame. Just truth.

That insight didn't erase the pain, but it opened the door to grace.

Overcome Blame due to Unspoken Expectations

Blame can feel justified, even comforting, when we're hurt or disappointed. But beneath most blame lies an unspoken expectation: something we assumed, hoped, or needed but never clearly communicated. This chapter invites you to move beyond resentment by turning inward with clarity and compassion. True empowerment begins when we stop waiting for others to change, and start owning what we can shift ourselves.

Reflect

Reflection helps you uncover the hidden roots of resentment. Often, where blame lingers, there was an unspoken expectation, of behavior, recognition, or reciprocity, that was never clearly voiced. Blame can protect us from vulnerability, but it also keeps us from moving forward.

- Where in your life are you still blaming someone else for your pain, stagnation, or unmet needs?

- What assumptions or expectations did you carry without ever articulating them, even to yourself?

- Where did those expectations come from: were they inherited from family, shaped by culture, or rooted in fear?

Journaling Prompt: *What expectations have I been holding in silence, and what would shift if I spoke them clearly or released them entirely?*

Reframe

Reframing allows you to move from blame to accountability, not as self-blame, but as self-liberation. Blame may soothe the ego, but it stunts evolution. Naming your part with compassion doesn't mean you excuse others; it means you choose growth over stagnation.

- Blame may feel easier, but it blocks transformation. Accountability restores momentum.

- Owning your role is not the same as excusing theirs. It's reclaiming your authorship over your next chapter.

- Expectations that go unspoken often become resentments. Communication brings clarity, and with it, freedom.

Mantra: *I release blame, speak my needs clearly, and reclaim my power with compassion.*

Reconnect

Reconnection is the practice of stepping back into your own agency. When you stop waiting for others to read your mind or meet your unspoken standards, you return to yourself. Grounded in truth, you can begin again, not from frustration, but from clarity.

- **Identify What's Within Your Control**
  Choose an area where you feel disappointed. List every factor you can influence, especially the uncomfortable ones.

- **Practice Compassionate Self-Inquiry**
  Ask: "What could I do differently moving forward, for my own peace, power, and clarity?"

- **Ground in Empowering Affirmations**
  Speak truth to your experience and growth:
  – I release blame and reclaim my voice.
  – I hold myself accountable with love, not judgment.
  – I am the author of my life, and I choose to write with clarity.

Affirmation: *I let go of silent expectations, take ownership of my needs, and lead my life with conscious clarity.*

Final Thought: Trade Blame for Brave Ownership

Blame builds walls.
Ownership opens doors.

Blame circles the wound.
Accountability begins the healing.

It takes courage to look within,
to face the mirror without defense.
To see not fault, but opportunity,
not shame, but invitation.

When you meet your mistakes with mercy,
they become teachers, not chains.
When you stand in your truth,
you no longer need control to feel strong.

Growth replaces guilt.
Peace replaces pride.

This is Sovereign Living.

RESENTMENT TO RADICAL FORGIVENESS

"Hurt people hurt people. That's how pain patterns get passed on, generation after generation. Break the chain today. Meet anger with sympathy, contempt with compassion, cruelty with kindness. Greet grimaces with smiles. Forgive and forget about finding fault. Love is the weapon of the future."
~ Yehuda Berg

Pain echoes through generations when left unhealed. It creates emotional residue, quiet but heavy. And when resentment takes root, it doesn't just affect the relationship that caused it; it begins to dim every part of our lives.

Radical forgiveness isn't about letting someone off the hook. It's about letting yourself off the hook, and releasing the emotional bondage that keeps you anchored to a past that no longer serves you. It's choosing peace over punishment. Wholeness over hurt.

My Story: Forgiveness Begins With Truth

Years after my divorce, I realized that although I had moved forward logistically, with a new home, a new chapter, and new rhythms, I was still tethered emotionally. The estrangement from two of my children lingered like a low-grade hum in my body, sometimes barely audible, other times unbearably loud.

In a moment of stillness, I decided to write. Not to explain or defend, but to forgive, and to ask for forgiveness. I sat with pen and paper and wrote four letters: one to my former husband, and one to each of my three children.

The first drafts were laced with justification, even subtle self-protection. But I paused. Rewrote. Let my Heart lead. And when I wrote to Maddie, the words came through with clarity and truth. The letter read, in part:

"My dearest Maddie, God's gift to me, my prayer answered, my teacher, my mirror, my conscience, and my best friend.

Please forgive me for any and all injustices I have caused you; known and unknown.

Please forgive me for the fear and uncertainty you carried through the divorce.

Please forgive me for asking you to shoulder burdens that were never yours to bear.

Please forgive me for the times you were caught between two worlds.

Most of all, please forgive me for placing you in the position of the family glue."

I intended them as a private ritual, words to release and then burn. But with Maddie, I knew the words needed to reach her. Not just energetically. Physically.

On Thanksgiving morning, we walked together along Zuma Beach. I handed her the letter. We sat quietly as she read it, the waves steady behind us. Tears welled in her eyes.

"You have no idea how much I needed this," she whispered.

And in that moment, I understood: my honesty gave her something she'd been holding out for, not answers, but *acknowledgment*.

Walls that had quietly divided us softened. Our connection began to mend, not because I fixed anything, but because I finally *owned everything*.

Healing Through Humble Acknowledgment

Healing doesn't always come through confrontation; sometimes, it begins with quiet acknowledgment. Forgiveness is not about denying the hurt, but about deciding that pain will no longer own your energy. When you humbly acknowledge the ways you've been wounded, or may have wounded others, you create space for freedom, not just for them, but for yourself. This chapter is about releasing resentment, softening the grip of blame, and reclaiming your peace through grace and truth.

Reflect

Reflection helps you name the weight you've been carrying, the pain, the silence, the unresolved story. Acknowledging where you've held anger, disappointment, or grief isn't about blame; it's about truth. Healing often begins not with fixing the past, but with seeing it clearly.

- Who do you still carry pain or anger toward, even if you've never voiced it aloud?

- What apology are you still waiting to receive, or still too guarded to give?

- How did unspoken expectations or unprocessed emotions contribute to the breakdown or lingering pain?

Journaling Prompt: *What am I still holding onto, and what would healing look like if I acknowledged it, without needing to be right?*

Reframe

Reframing invites you to see forgiveness not as weakness, but as strength. Humble acknowledgment doesn't erase the past; it empowers you to stop living in reaction to it. You can honor your pain and still choose peace. Forgiveness is not about the other person; it's a decision to give *yourself* back to yourself.

- Forgiveness doesn't mean forgetting. It means releasing the hold the past has on your energy.

- Your peace is more valuable than being proven right.

- You can honor your grief while choosing to rise; these things are not mutually exclusive.

Mantra: *I can carry truth and tenderness at the same time. I forgive to set myself free.*

Reconnect

Reconnection is the act of moving your healing from intention into embodiment. Through quiet rituals, honest expression, and emotional release, you begin to reclaim your energy. Whether or not the other person ever acknowledges their part, you can still choose to close the chapter with grace.

- **Write the Unsent Letter**
  Say everything, without filter, without fear. You don't need to send it. Just let the truth be spoken.

- **Engage in a Forgiveness Ritual**
  Use prayer, meditation, ocean, fire, or time in nature to symbolically release what no longer needs to be held.

- **Repeat the Ho'oponopono Prayer**
  Speak daily, slowly, with presence:
  – "I'm sorry." "Please forgive me." "Thank you." "I love you."

- **Visualize Releasing Resentment**
  Close your eyes. See yourself handing the weight back to the earth, to God, to the sea. Reclaim your energy.

- **Offer Yourself Grace**
  The grace you long to give or receive, start there. Begin with you.

Affirmation: *I release what no longer serves, forgive with humility, and reclaim my peace with love and grace.*

Final Thought: Forgive to Be Free

Resentment is a quiet poison.
It hardens the Heart and clouds the mind.
It steals the softness that love once knew.

Forgiveness is not forgetting.
It is remembering without being ruled by memory.
It is releasing the story so your soul can breathe again.

Radical forgiveness asks for courage,
to see your pain without clinging to it,
to name the wound without weaponizing it,
to love yourself enough to let go.

Forgive them, not to erase their part,
but to free yourself from the weight of the past.
Forgive yourself, for the times you stayed too long
or couldn't yet rise.

Let grace become your practice.
This is how you return to peace.

This is Sovereign Living.

REJECTION TO ACCEPTANCE

*"If they want to leave... let them.
If they choose someone else... let them.
If they don't support you... let them.
If they don't invite you... let them.
Stop wasting your energy trying
to control or change other people.
Let them show who they really
are. And then YOU can
choose what you do next."*
~ Mel Robbins

Rejection is never easy, especially when it comes from someone you love. But it's also not always personal. Sometimes it's a reflection of unmet needs, misaligned energy, or an unspoken mismatch in how joy is expressed and experienced.

Rejection stings most when it feels like a mirror of inadequacy. But what if it's really an invitation to return to yourself, to a version of you that's been buried beneath exhaustion, responsibility, or quiet resentment?

My Story: When Awareness Sparks Renewal

For years, I couldn't understand why my first husband rarely seemed eager for one-on-one time. I planned romantic trips, anniversaries, and dinner dates, only to be met with indifference, or worse, subtle resistance.

I interpreted it as disinterest in *me*. And it hurt.

One evening, while discussing marital strengths and weakness with a boyfriend, also divorced, he offered a reflection that stopped me in my tracks: "Maybe he simply enjoyed himself more when the kids were around. Maybe being alone together felt stressful instead of joyful."

His words hit like a wave. Not cruel, just clarifying. *Could it be true?*

As I sat with that possibility, I realized something: the playful, light-hearted version of myself had dimmed. Under the weight of raising three children, building a career, managing a home, I had become competent, dependable... and a little serious. Somewhere along the way, I traded spontaneity for structure. I traded fun for function.

In trying to do everything *right*, I had slowly lost the version of myself who once laughed easily, danced freely, flirted boldly, and leaned into the joy of just *being*.

And maybe my husband hadn't been rejecting me, but mourning that earlier version of *us*.

That realization wasn't about blame. It was about awareness. And in that awareness came acceptance, not of the situation alone, but of myself. I needed to rediscover the parts of me that made life feel vibrant, not just for a partner, but for my own wholeness.

Rejection can be a painful mirror. But if we look with honest eyes, it can reflect back the parts of ourselves we're ready to reclaim.

Returning to the Self You Left Behind

In the process of managing responsibilities, surviving heartbreak, or adapting to expectations, we often lose parts of ourselves, the joyful, playful, unfiltered expressions that once felt natural. But those parts aren't gone; they're waiting for permission to return. Reclaiming your lost self is not about going back, but about making room for the parts of you that never stopped longing to be seen, honored, and lived again.

Reflect

Reflection allows you to examine where and why certain aspects of your authentic self were set aside. Sometimes what we call rejection is actually redirection, a mirror showing us where we've disconnected from our own aliveness. In seeking to be accepted, have you abandoned parts of your truest self?

- Think of a time you felt rejected. Was it really about your worth, or about a dynamic that had naturally shifted?
- What part of yourself have you silenced or hidden to survive the demands of life, or to fit into someone else's expectations?
- Can you sense a version of yourself more creative, curious, lighthearted, still waiting to come forward?

Journaling Prompt: *What version of myself have I tucked away to stay safe, and how might I begin to welcome them home?*

Reframe

Reframing invites you to shift the narrative around loss and rejection. These experiences don't always signify failure; they can signal misalignment, or the call to reintegrate parts of yourself you've ignored. Reconnection isn't about fixing yourself; it's about becoming curious again about who you are, and who you're still becoming.

- Rejection is often a sign of misalignment, not a reflection of your unworthiness.
- The pain of losing someone or something may reflect a deeper loss of joy, creativity, spontaneity within yourself.
- Coming home to yourself begins with curiosity, not control. Be willing to rediscover rather than redesign.

Mantra: *I am not broken. I am simply returning to parts of myself I forgot were worthy of love.*

Reconnect

Reconnection is the active choice to reawaken joy, softness, and curiosity. It's about restoring connection to the self you once celebrated, not by changing everything, but by honoring small invitations to play, express, and feel again. And when in relationship, it's about noticing together what's been lost, and what's worth reviving.

- **Reclaim Joyful Parts of Yourself**
  Bring back an old passion: dancing, journaling, singing, painting, spontaneous movement. Let joy be reason enough.

- **Create Space Daily for Aliveness**
  Even in small ways, invite your lost self back into your routines. Light a candle. Walk barefoot. Laugh out loud.

- **If in Relationship, Revisit the Dynamic**
  Ask together: "What feels alive?" "What feels missing?" "What small rituals or memories might we bring back, or reinvent?"

- **Practice Radical Self-Acceptance**
  Welcome your past, your complexity, your becoming. Then offer that same grace outward, to others finding their way home too.

Affirmation: *I return to myself with love. Every part of me is welcome here, joyful, tender, and whole.*

Final Thought: Return to Yourself Before You Reach for Another

Rejection can feel like loss,
but often it is redirection,
a sacred mirror revealing where
you've drifted from your own light.

Acceptance is not surrender.
It is Sovereignty.
It is the moment you stop chasing validation
and start coming home to yourself.

You don't need to convince anyone to stay.
You only need to remember who you are
when you stop performing for belonging.

Let those who cannot meet your truth fall away.
Their absence makes room for self-love to return.

Return to the parts of you that once laughed easily,
loved boldly, and trusted deeply.
They are still waiting, radiant and ready to rise again.

This is not the end of your story.
It is the rediscovery of your essence.

This is Sovereign Living.

Pro Tip:
If you're ready to go deep with letting go, pick up *The Let Them Theory* by Mel Robbins. Her book offers a clear and actionable framework for freeing yourself from the burden of trying to control others. It teaches you to accept what you cannot change and instead focus your energy on your own choices, boundaries, and growth.

Part Five

PARENTING
RAISING SOULS, NOT JUST CHILDREN

Parenting is not a role; it is a spiritual practice in love, presence, and evolution. It is where our deepest wounds meet our greatest teachers, and where the sacred art of raising another begins with raising ourselves.

In **Parenting Begins at Birth to Parenting Begins at Conception**, you awaken to the truth that soul connection precedes physical arrival, that our children choose us as mirrors and guides long before we meet.

In **Birth Order to Balanced Being**, you learn to see each child through the lens of their unique position in the family story, not as a label, but as a language of love. You discover how awareness of birth order can bring harmony, how balance can replace comparison, and how attunement can transform parenting into presence.

Absent to Present invites you to slow down, to trade distraction for devotion, and to let love be felt, not just performed. Through **Transactional Relationship to Emotional Warmth**, you move from managing behavior to nurturing connection. **Parenting for Control to Parenting to Empower** reminds you that true authority is not force, but influence born of respect and emotional safety.

In **Parenting Others to Parenting Yourself**, you come to see that your inner child is the first one who needs reparenting, that healing yourself is how you free your lineage. **About Me to About You** invites humility and curiosity, turning projection into understanding.

And in **Lemons to Lemonade**, you learn to transform challenges into growth, finding sweetness even in the sour seasons. **Out-law to In-law** celebrates expansion, the shift from family by blood to family by choice, where love widens to include those who love our children.

Parenting, at its highest expression, is not about perfection; it is about presence. It is the practice of raising Sovereign souls, guided not by fear or control, but by grace, growth, and unconditional love.

PARENTING BEGINS AT BIRTH TO PARENTING BEGINS AT CONCEPTION

*"Making the decision to
have a child is momentous,
it is to decide forever to
have your Heart go walking
around outside your body."*
~ Elizabeth Stone

Most of us believe parenting begins the moment we first hold our baby in our arms. But the truth is far more sacred: parenting begins at conception.

Every thought, every meal, every emotion during pregnancy sends a message to the soul growing inside. The womb is not just a physical environment; it is the baby's first classroom. A container for love, fear, joy, and intuition.

Even before birth, we are already shaping how our child will learn to feel safe, to trust, to love, and to receive love in return.

Science tells us this. Ancient wisdom confirms it. But most powerfully, our *own* stories reflect it if we are willing to look closely.

My Story: Birthing Three Souls and Learning the Soul Contracts

When I was pregnant with each of my children, I felt deeply content. I nourished myself well (minus a few late-night pints of ice cream!), moved my body gently, and relished the miracle of life blooming within.

Sure, there were worries: *Would we have enough space? Would I be a good mom?* But overall, I loved being pregnant. Delivery, however, was another story.

My first child, was two weeks late and over nine pounds. She turned face-up during labor which is a serious complication. My doctor gave me two options: follow his exact instructions or prepare for an emergency C-section. Terrified, I chose to trust. After one of the most intense experiences of my life, she arrived: screaming, vibrant, radiant.

My second, Max, was to be induced early. During labor, the umbilical cord wrapped around his neck. I froze. My doctor moved with grace, unwrapping the cord like a master. And then: "It's a happy, healthy baby boy!" We named him Max David; *David* to honor my grandfather, a *pillar of courage*.

My third, Madison, arrived with ease. We chose to induce her two weeks early to keep her under nine pounds. She seemed ready, eager, even, to meet the world. No complications. No fear. Just a calm, steady flow. She literally bounced out. We named her Madison, like the mermaid in the movie *Splash*. She is our gift from God; *strong and mighty*. We call her Maddie.

A funny thing happened after her birth. My uncle Bob, my mother's brother, said, "I like how you named her after our childhood home, 222 Madison Avenue." I smiled and agreed. It hadn't been a conscious choice, but perhaps deep in my memory, there lived those joyful, playful visits to my mother's family. Maybe Madison was always meant to be.

At the time, I saw these stories as memories. But I now know: they were soul blueprints.

Years later, during a painful post-divorce period, a

deeper heartbreak arrived, one I never could have prepared for. Two of my three children had pulled away, leaving an emptiness that felt endless. The grief didn't just hurt; it hollowed me, echoing through my chest like a prayer unanswered.

After a healing Kundalini Yoga class, my teacher Susan Shaner approached gently and asked what was troubling me. I opened my Heart. She listened, and then offered something that changed everything: "Trust in universal law and the unbreakable energy that exists between a mother and her children."

She asked me about each of my pregnancies. When I shared them, she said: "Each of those births mirrors the soul contract you have with each child. Your firstborn had to be turned, just as your relationship with her may require careful navigation. Your second was suffocating; you had to create space for him to breathe. And your third came easily, because her soul wanted to stay close."

I was stunned. But I *knew* she was right. I wept. I released. From that moment on, I chose love. I visualized reunification. I trusted divine timing.

And slowly… one by one… my children have returned, each in their own way, to a new relationship with me. The bond was never broken, only resting, patient for love's return. This is the miracle of parenting from the soul.

How to Parent From the Soul. Beginning at Conception

Parenting from the soul doesn't begin at birth; it begins with awareness. It begins at conception, or even before, in the quiet agreement between souls. This chapter invites you to view parenting not as a task, but as a calling; not as control, but as communion. Whether you are preparing to parent, currently raising a child, or healing your own upbringing, this is your invitation to soften, deepen, and return to the sacred root of connection.

Reflect

To parent from the soul, begin by turning inward. Our early imprints often echo forward into the way we relate to our children. The emotional and energetic conditions surrounding your own conception and early life matter, not as something to judge, but as something to gently witness. Awareness opens the door to transformation.

- What were the emotional and physical circumstances surrounding your own birth? Were you planned, welcomed, unexpected, celebrated, or something else?

- How did your caregivers bond with you in your earliest years? Where was there presence or absence?

- If you are already a parent, what emotions surfaced before your child's birth? What hopes or fears shaped your first connection?

Journaling Prompt: *What were the circumstances surrounding your own birth? Ask your mother, or someone who knew her. What emotions, challenges, or blessings were present? How might those early conditions echo in your current relationships, especially with your child (or future child)?*

Reframe

Reframing allows you to see parenting not as a role to perform, but as a sacred relationship to tend. Children are not blank slates; they are wise, whole beings who arrive with a soul path of their own. You are not here to shape them into something. You are here to walk with them, to witness, and to be shaped in return.

- Parenting begins not at birth, but at the soul's decision to come through you.
- Your child chose you, not by accident, but by alignment.
- Every challenge is an invitation to look inward. What in you is being asked to heal, soften, or evolve?

Insight Practice: *Parenting doesn't begin in the delivery room; it begins with the soul's invitation to come through you. Your child chose you. Can you choose them back, fully, with your presence and your Heart?*

Reconnect

Reconnection reminds us that love is never lost. No matter the story, no matter the strain, the soul bond remains, waiting to be remembered, restored, and re-rooted in presence. You can reconnect in silence, in ritual, in word, or in intention. You don't need permission. You only need willingness.

- **Write a Letter**
  To your child (born or unborn), or to your mother. Speak truth. Offer gratitude. Release resentment. Say what needs to be said, even if it's never sent.

- **Create Sacred Space for Connection**
  Light a candle. Sit with a photo. Hold your Heart. Breathe in the knowing that love is still here.

- **Speak Soul to Soul**
  Out loud or in stillness, speak to the bond. Acknowledge what was, what is, and what you trust can still become.

Affirmation: *I honor the sacred soul bond between us, timeless, wise, and guided by love. I trust that what is meant to heal will heal, and what is meant to grow will grow.*

Final Thought: Parenting Begins with a Soulful Yes

Parenting is not an event.
It is an awakening.
It begins long before birth.
It begins in a quiet agreement between souls:
I choose you.

From that moment, a sacred thread is woven.
A child is not just someone you raise.
They are someone you remember.
They are a mirror and a teacher.

Every heartbeat in the womb is a conversation.
Every prayer becomes part of their knowing.
The womb teaches them what love feels like.
Even when distance appears, love does not leave.

It waits beneath the silence.
Parenting is devotion, not perfection.
It is a continual yes to love and growth.

This is Sovereign Living.

BIRTH ORDER TO BALANCED BEING

"The greatest gift we can give our children is to see them, truly see them, for who they are."
~ Rachel Macy Stafford

Every child is born into a different emotional landscape, even within the same home.

Birth order doesn't define a child's destiny, but it does influence how they see themselves, relate to others, and express love. Each position in the family; firstborn, middle, youngest, or only, offers its own lessons in belonging, individuality, and self-worth.

Psychologists like Meri Wallace, Kevin Leman, and Frank Sulloway have long explored these dynamics, revealing how the order in which a child arrives often mirrors the roles they grow to embody. Awareness of these patterns can help parents nurture balance, celebrating individuality without comparison.

My Story: The Family Template

When one of my nieces confided in her mother, saying she wouldn't speak to her if she ever left her father, I felt an old ache rise within me. Her words echoed moments from my own story and reflected dynamics I had lived through in my family. In that moment, I realized the pattern: a firstborn child's loyalty runs deep. The eldest often holds a silent contract with the parent who "stays," measuring love through constancy and performance.

As a firstborn myself, I understood the unspoken rule: success, stability, and doing things "right" are sacred. When a parent breaks from that script, even in pursuit of truth or healing, the firstborn feels betrayed. They see not courage, but collapse. This insight didn't erase the pain, but it brought clarity. I could finally see the emotion beneath the reaction, not rejection, but disappointment. Not anger, but grief.

My cousin and I often laugh at how our families mirror each other: three children, same sexes, same birth order; girl, boy, girl, each two years apart. Our sons, the middle children, are driven, disciplined, and endlessly social, building empires, chasing purpose, and surrounding themselves with brothers of the Heart. Beneath their confidence lies a tenderness they rarely reveal. We often joke that they'll make the best husbands, fluent in the language of women after growing up between two very different sisters.

And our youngest daughters? They embody the spirit of YOLO, you only live once, and they live it well. Bright, social, endlessly curious, they gather people the way light gathers warmth. Their partners meet their "uh-oh" moments not with criticism, but with laughter and love.

It's only now, reflecting on these patterns, that I see how closely they echo my family of origin: three children again, girl, boy, girl, two years apart. I was the firstborn, always the perfectionist. My brother Peter was the steady empath, sensing what others could not express. And my sister Chrissy was the spirited, social soul whose joy filled every room.

Our families, it seems, are living mandalas, repeating forms that reveal not just who we are, but who we're here to become. When we begin to see the pattern, we no longer judge it. We learn from it.

Firstborns: The Pathfinders

The firstborn enters a world of structure and high expectations. Parents are often new to the role, careful, attentive, and by the book. This early intensity shapes the first child into a natural leader: responsible, reliable, and often perfectionistic. They thrive on approval, achievement, and a sense of control. Yet beneath the drive to "get it right" can live a fear of failure and a longing for ease.

Parents can support firstborns by softening the pressure to perform, celebrating effort over outcome, and reminding them that love is not earned, it's given.

Common strengths: leadership, diligence, reliability
Potential challenges: rigidity, self-criticism, fear of mistakes

Middle Children: The Bridge Builders

Caught between the "trailblazer" and the "baby," middle children often learn diplomacy early. They become peacemakers, negotiators, and connectors, social beings who find belonging in friendship and collaboration. Because attention is divided at home, middles may develop independence and empathy, seeking validation beyond the family. Still, they can struggle with invisibility, wondering where they truly fit.

Parents can help by making space for their voice, validating their uniqueness, and celebrating their role as harmonizers, not just mediators.

Common strengths: adaptability, empathy, teamwork
Potential challenges: people-pleasing, self-doubt, feeling unseen

Youngest Children: The Free Spirits

The youngest arrives in a home that's already in motion; the rules are looser, the parents more relaxed. They often learn charm as a strategy for attention and bring humor and lightness to the family dynamic. Naturally social and adventurous, they're the ones who keep joy alive. But with fewer expectations, they can grow dependent on their charm or resist responsibility.

Parents can empower the youngest by entrusting them with real responsibilities and acknowledging their capability, not just their charisma.

Common strengths: creativity, playfulness, optimism
Potential challenges: attention-seeking, avoidance of accountability

Only Children: The Old Souls

Without siblings to share space or resources, only children live as "super-firstborns." They receive deep parental focus, and with it, high expectations. Mature for their age, they often mirror adult sensibilities and carry a strong inner drive for excellence. But constant attention can create pressure and perfectionism.

Parents can help by encouraging play, peer connection, and flexibility, reminding the only child that mistakes are part of growth, not a failure of worth.

Common strengths: maturity, focus, self-discipline
Potential challenges: over-responsibility, isolation, perfectionism

Patterns don't define us; they invite us to see ourselves more clearly. Within every family lives a quiet choreography: the one who leads, the one who harmonizes, the one who brings light, the one who stands alone. Each position carries its own wisdom, its own wound, its own way of seeking love.

When we begin to see these roles not as labels but as living energies, we soften. We meet our children and our own inner child with deeper compassion. What follows are gentle reflections on the paths each child walks and how we, as parents, can walk beside them with greater balance and grace.

Parenting with Awareness

Birth order doesn't define who your child will become, but it does reveal where love and attention want to flow. Each child is shaped by the ecosystem they're born into: the expectations, comparisons, and quiet dynamics that unfold between siblings and parents. Awareness helps us see these invisible patterns not as problems to fix, but as invitations to balance what may have unconsciously tilted toward performance, invisibility, or freedom without roots.

As parents, our task is not to mold our children to fit an archetype, but to see and support the soul beneath the pattern. When your oldest carries too much responsibility, teach them that rest is a form of strength. When your middle child blends into the background, remind them that their voice matters. When your youngest leads with laughter, help them find depth beneath the delight. And when your only child bears the weight of your hopes, remind them they're allowed to simply be.

Parenting with awareness means choosing presence over pattern. It's the art of attunement, of meeting each child where they are, not where you think they should be. Awareness is love in motion. And when we parent with that kind of love, we don't just raise capable children; we nurture emotionally balanced, Sovereign beings who know how to belong to themselves and to the world.

Reflect

Every child arrives with their own rhythm, and birth order often plays the first note in that song. Begin by observing, without judgment, the roles that naturally emerge within your family.

- How does your **oldest** carry responsibility or strive for perfection?
- Does your **middle child** seek harmony or hide in the background?
- Does your **youngest** charm, distract, or play to be seen?
- Does your **only child** crave both closeness and autonomy?

Then, turn that awareness inward.

- What was your own place in the family story?
- How might those early dynamics still shape your parenting today?

Journaling Prompt: *How does my birth order influence the way I parent? What roles have I unconsciously assigned to my children, and what new story am I ready to create for each of them?*

Reframe

Birth order doesn't define destiny; it simply reveals where balance is asking to be restored.

- For the **firstborn**, ease the pressure to perform. Let them feel safe in imperfection.

- For the **middle child**, celebrate their individuality. Let them shine in their own light.

- For the **youngest**, pair freedom with responsibility. Teach that joy and accountability can coexist.

- For the **only child**, nurture both solitude and connection. Show them the beauty of interdependence.

As you begin to reframe your understanding, remember: awareness is love made visible. Seeing your child clearly, not through comparison but through compassion, transforms parenting from reaction to relationship.

Empowering Question: *What if my role isn't to fix or equalize my children, but to love them in alignment with who they naturally are?*

Reconnect

Balance begins in presence. Parenting isn't about correction; it's about connection, noticing when one child needs affirmation, another needs space, and all need your calm.

- Give your **oldest** permission to play.

- Give your **middle child** a moment that's entirely theirs.

- Give your **youngest** a turn to lead.
- Give your **only child** time to simply be.

And give yourself grace. Parenting is a practice of attunement, imperfect, evolving, and endlessly redemptive.

Affirmation: *I honor each child's rhythm and role. I release comparison and welcome balance. I parent not by order, but by Heart.*

Final Thought: See the Soul, Not the Sequence

Your children are not their order; they are their essence.
They are not defined by who came first or last.
They are shaped by the love that surrounds them.
By the space you create for them to unfold.
By the freedom you give them to grow into themselves.

When you look beyond labels, something softens.
The responsible one.
The peacemaker.
The wild one.
The independent one.

These are not identities; they are survival roles.
Beneath them lives a soul longing to be seen.

Parenting with awareness is not about managing roles.
It is about giving each spirit room to breathe.
To stumble and rise in their own timing.
Because love, when seen clearly, has no order at all.

This is Sovereign Living.

ABSENT TO PRESENT

"Children spell love... T-I-M-E."
~ Dr. Anthony P. Witham

"Be here now." Three simple words made legendary by Ram Dass, and perhaps the most profound parenting advice of all time. Presence is what our children crave most, not perfection or performance. Just us. Fully here. Fully human. Fully with them.

If you've never read *Be Here Now*, this quote from Alfred D. Souza offers a similar truth:

> "For a long time, it seemed to me that life was about to begin, real life. But there was always some obstacle in the way, something to be gotten through first... Then life would begin. At last, it dawned on me: these obstacles were my life."

When we stop waiting for the "right time," the "perfect day," or the "cleared schedule," we begin to truly live. More importantly, we begin to truly love, in the moment, as we are.

Our greatest gift is time.

My Story: From Multitasking Mom to Present Grandmother

As a working mother, I made every effort to be there for my children: ballet recitals, lacrosse games, open houses, fundraisers. My calendar overflowed with good intentions.

But if I'm honest, I was often split in two, physically present, mentally scattered.

Dinner prep blurred into work calls. Homework help competed with emails. My kids would whisper or wave for my attention while I juggled ten things at once.

They knew they were loved. They were supported, celebrated, and seen to the best of my ability at the time. But if I could speak to that version of myself now, I would gently say: *"Put the cooking knife down. Let the call go to voicemail. Turn to your child, look them in the eye, and be here."*

Because love isn't measured in meals cooked or errands completed. It's measured in moments: sacred, present, fully embodied moments.

Today, as a mother of grown children and a grandmother, I bring presence as my offering. No more multitasking. No more rushing. Just open eyes, open ears, and an open Heart. It has changed everything.

Cultivating True Presence With Your Children and Grandchildren

True presence is one of the most powerful gifts you can offer a child. It's not about doing more; it's about *being* more fully with. In a world full of distractions and endless demands, presence says: "You matter. I'm here. And this moment is enough."

Reflect

Before we can be present with others, we must first become present with ourselves. Reflection helps us tune in to what matters most.

- Think back to a recent moment when you were truly present, no phone, no multitasking, just *being* with your child or grandchild. How did it feel?

- What memories have left the deepest imprint on your Heart? Often, it's not the big events, but the small, quiet, connected moments.

- Consider how your own childhood shaped your understanding of presence. Were you deeply seen? Or often overlooked?

Journaling Prompt: *When was the last time you were fully present with your child or loved one, undistracted, open-hearted? What made that moment meaningful? What gets in the way of presence for you now?*

Reframe

Presence isn't a luxury; it's love in its purest, most healing form. Let go of the belief that doing more means loving more.

- Productivity does not equal love. Presence is not something extra; it is the essence of connection.

- You don't have to perform, fix, or entertain. Your being is more important than your doing.

- Even brief, intentional presence can be powerful. A few minutes of genuine connection can outweigh hours of distracted time.

Empowering Question: *What would shift if I believed that my presence, without perfection or performance, is enough?*

Mantra: *My presence is my greatest gift. Love flows not from what I do, but from who I am when I'm fully here.*

Reconnect

To cultivate presence, begin with small, sacred choices. Let love live in your routines, your rituals, your everyday moments.

- Choose one simple ritual to share: a morning hug, a walk, a screen-free dinner. Make it sacred by showing up fully for it.

- Communicate with intention. If you must step away, honor your word when you return. Trust is built through follow-through.

- Listen with your whole being. Don't rush to fix. Let them feel seen, heard, and safe in your quiet attention.

Affirmation: *My presence is love. This moment is enough. I choose connection over perfection.*

Final Thought: Be Here Now

Presence is the purest form of love.
It says without words, you matter.
I see you.
I'm here.

Children don't need perfection.
They need our eyes, hands, and laughter.
They need us unguarded and unhurried.
Presence becomes rebellion in a distracted world.

It teaches children to slow down.
It teaches them to listen and belong.
They won't remember every meal or trip.
They will remember how your face lit up.

They will remember your hand in theirs.
And your voice saying, I'm proud of you.
Presence chooses now over later.
This moment is enough.

This is Sovereign Living.

TRANSACTIONAL RELATIONSHIP TO EMOTIONAL WARMTH

"I've learned that people will forget what you said, people will forget what you did, but people will never forget how you made them feel."
~ Maya Angelou

In a world that values doing over being, it's easy to fall into the rhythm of relationships defined by checklists and logistics. We feed, clothe, schedule, and guide our children, and sometimes forget to simply love them with our presence.

Emotional warmth isn't about what we provide. It's about how we show up.

We may check every box and still miss the moment that matters most: the feeling of being truly seen, truly heard, and unconditionally loved.

My Story: A Moment That Changed Me Forever

While consulting for Modern Elder Academy, I met Mark Goulston, a psychiatrist and bestselling author known for his calm, NPR-level presence and penetrating insight.

He asked me a question that felt like an arrow straight to my chest: "What is your relationship with your children?"

I shared the truth: after my divorce, I had become estranged from two of my three children. It was painful, disorienting, and something I carried quietly, beneath my professional success.

Mark responded with a sentence that has never left me: "It's a shame how the transactional world killed off the best part of women."

He explained how women of our generation were the first to be told we could "have it all": careers, children, homes, and independence. But we weren't taught how to balance it. We became excellent at getting things done, but somewhere along the way, the emotional softness of mothering got buried under the weight of everything else.

I had poured myself into raising successful, well-adjusted children: meals prepared, clothes folded, schedules maintained. But I now realize: I loved them transactionally through doing. Not always through being.

I thought emotional warmth meant spotless homes, planned dinners, and achievements. It wasn't. It was my son who finally told me the truth. During a difficult moment post-marital separation, he said: "I don't feel emotionally connected to you."

I was gutted. How could that be, when I believed I had given him everything?

But I understand now: he didn't need everything. He needed *me*. Soft. Present. Undistracted. A sanctuary, not a supervisor.

How to Cultivate Emotional Warmth in Daily Life

Emotional warmth is the quiet, steady flame of connection. It doesn't require grand gestures, just presence, openness, and a Heart willing to soften. In our fast-paced world, cultivating emotional warmth is an act of love that deepens every relationship, one small moment at a time.

Reflect

Before we can offer emotional warmth to others, we must recognize where it may be missing, or gently buried beneath busyness and good intentions.

- Think of a time when you were physically present but emotionally distant, offering help, solutions, or tasks, but not Heart.

- Consider relationships where your attention may be divided. Are there patterns where your body shows up, but your presence does not?

- Notice how others respond when you slow down and truly see them. What shifts when you lead with empathy instead of efficiency?

Journaling Prompt: *In what ways have you shown up for others through action but not emotion? When has your attention been requested, but your Heart wasn't fully there? What might emotional warmth look like in those moments?*

Reframe

Emotional warmth isn't about doing more; it's about being present with more softness, sincerity, and attunement.

- Productivity is not intimacy. Being helpful is not the same as being emotionally available.
- True connection isn't measured in tasks completed; it's felt in safe, attuned presence.
- You don't have to fix everything. You only need to be *with* someone in their experience.

Mantra: *I don't need to have the answers. I just need to be here, with love, with presence, with warmth.*

Reconnect

Emotional warmth is rekindled in everyday moments. When we bring our full attention to another, without agenda, we create space for healing, closeness, and joy.

- Choose one person today. Offer five minutes of your full, undistracted attention. No phone. No advice. Just be there.
- Use eye contact, an open posture, or a gentle touch to communicate, "I'm with you."
- Ask a Heart-centered question: "How's your Heart today?" or "Is there anything you've been carrying alone?"

Affirmation: *My presence is enough. My warmth is healing. I choose connection over correction, love over performance.*

Final Thought: Choose Presence Over Performance

You don't have to do more.
You have to feel more.
Be more.
Soften more.

In a world obsessed with output,
love asks for something quieter: presence.
Not the perfect dinner or the solved problem.
Just you, open-hearted and fully here.
People don't remember the tasks you mastered.

They remember how you made them feel.
The tone of your voice.
The warmth in your gaze.
The safety in your silence.

Love is not in what you accomplish.
It is in how you show up.
Let your presence say,
You matter. I see you. I'm here.
Be the sanctuary they return to,
and the soul they remember.

This is Sovereign Living.

PARENTING FOR CONTROL TO PARENTING TO EMPOWER

"Effective Parenting 101: Teaching our children to control themselves is far more effective than trying to control our children.
Model, don't manipulate.
Lead, don't intimidate.
Support, don't shame.
Encourage, don't threaten.
Guide, don't punish.
Listen, don't lecture."

~ L.R. Knost

Parenting is not about molding children into perfect versions of ourselves. It is about seeing them clearly, loving them fiercely, and trusting them deeply as they unfold into who they are meant to be. True love in parenting is not control; it is the courage to let each child reveal their own rhythm, purpose, and light.

Our role is sacred: to protect, nourish, and guide, but not to own. To provide safety, not scripts. To teach self-trust instead of blind obedience. When we parent with awareness, we create a foundation strong enough for freedom to grow. Our task is not to shape perfection, but to cultivate belonging, resilience, and authenticity.

The trap is subtle. We say we want our children to be happy, yet our definition of "happy" often carries the weight of our own unfinished story. Our old wounds, unfulfilled dreams, and inherited fears can quietly lead us to control what was never ours to begin with: their journey. True parenting invites us to release attachment to outcomes and to honor the sacred truth that our children do not belong to us they belong to life itself.

My Story: From Soothing to Surrender

I remember holding each of my newborns against my chest, their tiny bodies trembling with emotion, their cries filling the room. My instinct was always to comfort, not to correct. To hold, not to hush. To soothe, not to separate. In those early moments, I learned that love begins not with words, but with presence, the steady heartbeat of reassurance that says, *you are safe here.*

Well-meaning voices often said, "Let them cry. They need to learn independence." But I knew in my soul that babies do not cry to manipulate; they cry to communicate. They cry because they need love, touch, and safety. I offered those things freely, without hesitation or apology. To me, their tears were not an inconvenience; they were a sacred language asking to be understood.

As my children grew, the world around me began to shift. Parenting culture started to glorify control: structured routines, rigid expectations, trophies, timelines, and tidy outcomes. Something inside me resisted. I could not measure love by charts or milestones, and I refused to believe that growth unfolds according to plans or deadlines. The Heart of parenting lives in connection, not compliance.

I chose a different path. While I stayed organized, involved, and deeply committed to setting my children up for success, I did not hover or micromanage their lives. I believed in equipping them, not enclosing them. I practiced guidance, not control. Rather than anticipating every challenge for them, I gave them room to try, stumble, rise, and learn who they were becoming. My role was to support their steps, not to script them.

Now, with time and wisdom on my side, I see with greater clarity. Our children are not our projects; they are our mirrors. They come through us, not for us. Our purpose is not to sculpt them into something beautiful, but to show them that they already are. Parenting, in its truest form, is not about shaping perfection; it is about remembering love.

Parenting to Empower, Not Control

True empowerment in parenting begins when we release the need to control and instead trust the wisdom, resilience, and individuality of our children. When we guide rather than dictate, model rather than demand, and listen rather than lecture, we raise humans who know their worth, trust their voice, and feel safe to grow.

Reflect

Parenting from empowerment requires self-awareness. Begin by noticing your own patterns of control and the beliefs that drive them.

- Reflect on times when you may have confused control with care. Was your response about their needs, or your fears?

- Ask yourself where you are offering true guidance, and where you might be projecting your own story or unhealed wounds.

- Notice how your child responds when you give them space versus when you try to steer the outcome.

Journaling Prompt: *Have I ever confused control with care? Where am I empowering my child and where might I be unintentionally silencing their voice to manage my own discomfort?*

Reframe

Let go of the illusion that being "in control" equals being a good parent. Real power lies in connection, trust, and emotional safety.

- Control feels tight, rigid, and fear-based. Empowerment feels open, curious, and compassionate.

- You don't have to be "right" all the time to be respected. Humility, listening, and mutual growth create true authority.

- When you model emotional regulation, curiosity, and self-trust, you teach by example, not force.

Empowering Question: *What would shift if I led with trust instead of fear? How might I parent differently if I believed my child's soul came with its own wisdom?*

Reconnect

Empowerment begins again in every moment we choose to show up differently, with softness, with humility, and with presence.

- **Revisit L.R. Knost's words**
  "When little people are overwhelmed by big emotions, it's our job to share our calm, not join their chaos." Let this guide your next hard moment.

- **Model emotional honesty**
  Apologize when needed, share your own learning, and allow your child to witness your growth.

- **Choose one daily moment to let them lead**
  Empower them to choose what they wear, how they solve a problem, what they want to talk about. Show them you trust them.

Affirmation: *I choose connection over control. I am here to guide, not to mold. My child's wholeness matters more than my comfort.*

Final Thought: Let Them Become Who They Already Are

You are not here to script their story.
You are here to witness it.
To marvel at the mystery that chose
to come through you.

Your role is not to sculpt, but to see.
Not to control, but to cultivate.
Not to perfect, but to protect what is already whole.

Control is fear disguised as love.
It whispers that shaping them will keep them safe.
But safety born of control creates dependence,
not trust.

True empowerment says, I believe in your wisdom.
Even when it differs from mine.

Let your guidance be gentle.
Let your words build, not bind.
Let your love create space, not shrink their becoming.

Parenting is not ownership.
It is stewardship.

This is Sovereign Living.

PARENTING OTHERS TO PARENTING YOURSELF

"Hold the hand of the child that lives in your soul. For this child, nothing is impossible."
~ Paulo Coelho

Throughout life, many of us become caretakers; parenting siblings, partners, friends, coworkers. We become the emotional glue for those around us. The counselor. The steady one. The one who holds it all together.

This often begins in childhood, long before we have the language to explain it. Perhaps you were the eldest sibling. Perhaps you were a peacekeeper in a household filled with chaos. Perhaps you were simply "the responsible one." Somewhere along the way, your value became tied to protecting and managing the emotions of others.

But what if your greatest responsibility now... is to parent yourself? Imagine this: You, at five or six years old. Eyes wide. Heart open. Bursting with creativity, mischief, tenderness, and possibility. What would it look like to parent *that* child with as much love, consistency, and protection as you've given to everyone else?

My Story: From Caretaking to Compassionate Re-parenting

I think of my cousin Connie, the eldest of thirteen grandchildren, who, to this day, at over sixty years old, still feels a quiet responsibility to care for us all. That role was assigned to her early, as the "big cousin." It became an identity she never put down. No matter who she is in relation with she has an overwhelming sense she is responsible for over seeing her family, her parents, her children, her grandchildren, her work mates and the several hundred students at the private school she works at.

In my own life, I too became the one who held space for others. For my children, for my colleagues, for aging parents, for friends navigating their own storms. And while nurturing others is a beautiful calling, I eventually realized something essential was missing: I had neglected to parent *myself*.

It wasn't until I began exploring inner child work that I saw it clearly. When I pictured myself at six years old dancing in a bikini, barefoot on the sand, and with a head full of dreams, I realized, she's still inside me. She still needs love, safety, permission to dream, and permission to rest.

Parenting yourself is not self-indulgent. It is self-honoring. It is the root of Sovereignty.

How to Parent Yourself With Love and Presence

Before we can fully nurture others, we must first learn to nurture ourselves. Reparenting is the sacred act of tending to the unmet needs, forgotten dreams, and emotional wounds we've long carried. It's not about blame; it's about coming home to ourselves with compassion, clarity, and care.

Reflect

Self-parenting begins with courageous honesty. To love yourself well, you must first understand what you've been unconsciously carrying.

- Reflect on whether you've spent most of your life parenting others, meeting their needs while ignoring your own.

- Explore where that pattern may have begun. Was it modeled for you? Expected of you?

- Ask yourself: "What did I most long to receive as a child: attention, safety, encouragement, freedom?"

Journaling Prompt: *Have I spent most of my life parenting others before parenting myself? Where did that begin, and what did I most deeply need but never fully receive?*

Reframe

You are not here only to rescue or regulate others. You are here to be whole. To belong to yourself. To become your own safe place.

- Your worth is not dependent on how well you take care of everyone else. You are allowed to need care, too.

- Reparenting is not selfish; it is sacred. When you give yourself what you once lacked, you stop unconsciously demanding it from others.

- You can offer love, grace, and guidance to the younger version of you, anytime. That child still lives inside you, waiting to be seen.

Mantra: *I am not here to fix everyone. I am here to love and honor myself, just as I needed back then.*

Reconnect

Your inner child holds the key to joy, truth, and healing. When you reconnect with that part of yourself, you return to your essence.

- Close your eyes and picture yourself as a child. Where are they now? What do they want you to remember?

- Place a photo of your younger self somewhere visible. Let it be a gentle reminder that you are still becoming, and still deserving of tenderness.

- Do something this week just for them. Dance in the kitchen. Draw with crayons. Nap. Say no. Say yes. Whatever brings a spark of joy.

Affirmation: *I am a loving, present parent to myself. I honor my inner child's voice, protect their Heart, and choose joy without apology.*

Final Thought: The Parent You've Been Waiting For... Is You

You are worthy of your own tenderness.
There is no love more constant than
the one you offer yourself.
You have spent a lifetime holding others.
But the one who has waited the longest is you.

You are not broken.
You are becoming.
You are not late.
You are right on time.

The child within still waits for you.
She longs to hear,
"You're safe now."
"You're loved."
"You can rest."

Parenting yourself is sacred repair.
It ends old cycles of silence and self-abandonment.
It teaches love from the inside out.
Meet the you who is finally ready to come home.

This is Sovereign Living.

Pro Tip:

Keep a photo of your youngest, most joyful self somewhere visible, one that stirs a deep, emotional response in you. Let it remind you:

Affirmation: *I am making choices on behalf of her now. I am her protector, her voice, and her guide.*

ABOUT ME TO ABOUT YOU

"There is no love without humility. Holding space for another begins when you let go of your own need to be seen."
~ Bryant McGill

One of the most profound shifts in parenting, and in any conscious relationship, is the moment we stop making it about us and begin centering the needs, emotions, and perspectives of others.

When we release the urge to control, explain, or be understood, and instead lean in to listen, witness, and support, a sacred transformation occurs: People feel seen. Heard. Valued.

And in the presence of that kind of love, true connection takes root.

My Story: A Dance Between Letting Go and Letting Love In

In 2023, our family entered a season of celebration. Four weddings. Two new babies. And for the first time in years, no funerals.

After three consecutive years of loss, it felt as though the heavens had opened, sending us a wave of new beginnings. Each birth, each ceremony felt like a love letter from those we'd lost, reminding us that life continues, and joy returns.

One afternoon during a touch base call, my mother mentioned a family gathering she enjoyed in Naples, FL the evening before. My nephew and his fiancée were making final decisions for their upcoming wedding, including the song for the mother-son dance.

My mother casually remarked, "I feel like the song should be a dedication to the mother."

At first, I hadn't considered it that way. I remembered that at my own wedding, my mother-in-law had chosen "You Are the Sunshine of My Life" by Stevie Wonder for her dance with her son.

Back then, I just appreciated the sentiment. I never really thought about how meaningful that moment must have been for her.

Later that week, my son texted me: "Hey! I'm trying to pick the song we'd be dancing to at my wedding. I'm tied between two..."

"Landslide" the Dixie Chicks version
OR "Starting Over" by Chris Stapleton

"Landslide reminds me of you. I feel like you liked listening to it when we were younger. I like the lyrics, about the ebbs and flows of life and change."

"Starting Over… it kind of feels like our relationship has changed over the years, and now we're at a new point. I like the line 'nobody wins afraid of losing' and 'the hard roads are the ones worth choosing.'"

I sat with his words, and then I cried.

"Landslide" had been my silent companion during a time of deep transition. I could hear Stevie Nicks voice sweeping through my head: *"Can I handle the seasons of my life?"* And *"Well, I've been afraid of changin' 'cause I built my life around you."*

I had never heard of Chris Stapleton, let alone the song "Starting Over", but the title alone, paired with Max's thoughtful tribute, told me everything. It perfectly captured where we had landed: full circle, stronger, wiser, more open-hearted. In that moment, the song became more than music. It became a quiet homage to the journey we had walked, and who we had become.

I texted back: "Omg. Tears... Both choices are so thoughtful. I love that you remembered "Landslide". But yes, "Starting Over" is our story."

"Thank you for making me feel so special. I love you."

He replied simply: "Of course. I love you."

That was it. A sacred moment. A healing. A bridge between mother and son. Not because I planned it. But because I stepped back and let it be about him.

How to Practice the Shift from About Me to About You

True connection deepens when we learn to step out of the spotlight and hold space for others to shine. Moving from "about me" to "about you" is not about diminishing ourselves; it's about expanding our capacity for love, trust, and emotional generosity. This practice helps us tune into humility, release control, and honor the unfolding of someone else's path.

Reflect

Begin by noticing where your desire to help, direct, or be seen may unintentionally overshadow others.

- Where in your life do you feel the need to control outcomes, especially in relationships that matter most?
- Can you recall a moment when someone else needed the spotlight, but you found it hard to step back?
- Have you ever offered advice or solutions when someone simply needed presence and trust?

Journaling Prompt: *Where in my life do I default to control or visibility when what's truly needed is presence and support? How can I become more aware of those moments in real time?*

Reframe

Let go of the belief that stepping aside means stepping down. Centering others is not self-erasure; it's sacred trust.

- Their success, healing, or visibility is not a threat to your worth. Love expands when shared.
- Surrendering control isn't weakness; it's often the highest form of faith in another's path.
- Being right, being heard, or being the one in charge isn't always the goal. Sometimes the goal is simply to be *with*.

Empowering Question: *What if the most loving thing I could do in this moment is not to guide, but to trust, to listen, and to let go?*

Reconnect

Connection grows when we choose presence over power, curiosity over control, and humility over hierarchy.

- Identify a relationship that would benefit from more listening, more spaciousness, and less direction.
- Ask open-hearted questions like: "What do you need from me right now?" or "How can I support your truth, not my version of it?"
- Celebrate their autonomy. Even when their choices look different from yours, honor their wisdom, growth, and timing.

Affirmation: *I honor your path. I trust your timing. I release the need to lead and choose instead to love.*

Final Thought: Letting Them Lead

Love matures when it no longer needs to be right.
It grows quieter, wiser, softer.
It stops performing and starts trusting.

True love shines its light on others, not itself.
It steps back so another soul can rise.
It knows presence is greater than persuasion.

To love deeply is to honor another's timing.
To whisper, You've got this, and let them lead.

When you release the need to be understood,
you understand.
When you stop directing, you learn to walk beside.

Love becomes sacred when it stops
shaping and starts seeing.
When it honors without owning.
When it celebrates without centering itself.

Let them lead.
Let them live.
Let love evolve.

This is Sovereign Living.

LEMONS TO LEMONADE

"When life gives you lemons, make lemonade."
~ Elbert Green Hubbard

We've all heard this phrase tossed around, often offered when plans unravel or life delivers the unexpected. But when we pause to reflect, this isn't just a tired cliché; it's a masterclass in resilience.

A lemon, on its own, is sour and hard to swallow. But with water, sweetness, and care, it transforms into something refreshing and life-giving. Life's challenges work the same way.

This is a truth I especially love to share with children. The metaphor is simple, the message profound: optimism isn't denial; it's power. Teaching kids to transform disappointment into determination gives them a lifelong tool.

Because here's what's true: children don't just listen to our words, they absorb our energy. If we fall apart at every setback, they internalize that as normal. But if we pivot, adapt, and smile through the chaos, we show them how powerful they truly are.

My Story: The Road to Lemonade in the Sun

One spring break, we were all set for our annual escape to Florida. Sunshine, palm trees, and sandy toes awaited us, and this year, we had a bonus: my daughter's friend was coming along.

We arrived at LaGuardia early to beat an incoming storm, only to learn our flight was canceled, along with every other flight out of the Northeast. The airport became a whirlwind of panic and disappointment.

But I looked at my family and said what my soul knew was true: "Let's go. We're driving."

The kids lit up. We rented a minivan, loaded our bags, and drove *22 hours* straight to Naples, FL. Gas station snacks, music battles, silly games, and unexpected detours turned the journey into an adventure. And when the airline later offered a refund for our outbound flights and a discount on the return flight this was the cherry on top! Now we didn't have to drive the minivan rental back. We could now pay the drop off fee and fly back for less money!

On that snowy night, we could have gone home defeated. Instead, we made memories that will last a lifetime. We made lemonade.

How to Make Lemonade from Life's Lemons

Life doesn't always go as planned. But within every unexpected twist lies an opportunity, not just to adapt, but to grow, connect, and even thrive. Making lemonade is less about denying the sour moments and more about transforming them with creativity, humor, and Heart. This practice helps you turn setbacks into soulful stepping stones.

Reflect

To move forward with grace, start by acknowledging your initial reaction to life's disruptions, and the ripple effect it creates.

- Can you recall a time when your carefully laid plans unraveled? What emotion rose first: frustration, fear, surrender?

- How did you respond? How did your energy influence those around you, especially children or loved ones?

- What story did you tell yourself in that moment: "This always happens to me," or "Maybe this is a blessing in disguise"?

Journaling Prompt: *When was the last time life threw me a curveball? How did I respond, and what impact did that response have on those I love? What would I choose differently next time?*

Reframe

Flexibility isn't about giving up control; it's about learning to dance with change. Often, what feels like a loss is just the universe rerouting you toward something better.

- Life rarely follows the script, and sometimes the improvisation becomes the highlight.

- A canceled event might lead to spontaneous joy. A disappointment might reveal what truly matters.

- Your ability to pivot with grace teaches those around you that adaptability is a superpower.

Mantra: *This is not the end of the story; it's a plot twist. I trust something good can still grow here.*

Reconnect

Use life's disruptions as invitations to realign with joy, model resilience, and build deeper connection through shared problem-solving and laughter.

- Pause and ask: "What's the hidden opportunity in this moment?" "What memory might we be making instead?"
- Involve your family or loved ones in the solution. Turning lemons into lemonade is a team sport.
- Share the story of how things went sideways, and what came from it. Help others (and yourself) remember: every setback holds a seed of meaning.

Affirmation: *I meet life's lemons with open hands and a creative Heart. I choose to turn challenge into connection, and detours into discoveries.*

Final Thought: Where the Lemon Meets the Love

Life will hand you lemons.
Sometimes gently, sometimes by the bucketful.
You can resist them.
You can reach for the sugar.

It is never the event.
It is always your response.
Every sour twist holds sweetness.
Every bitter seed hides promise.

Pause when plans crumble.
Breathe before you react.
Smile if your Heart allows.
This is where alchemy begins.

Frustration softens into laughter.
Detours become new roads.
Joy rises through the rain.
Let the lemon meet the love.

This is Sovereign Living.

OUT-LAW TO IN-LAW

*"A mother gives you life,
a mother-in-law gives
you her life."*

~ *Amit Kalantri*

In many families, the term "in-law" carries with it an unspoken boundary, a subtle suggestion that this person is not quite *one of us*. But what if we shifted that perspective entirely? What if we saw in-laws not as outsiders, but as sacred additions to our circle, new Hearts, new stories, new souls choosing to love the ones we love?

We often speak of love as expansive. Let's live that truth by letting our families grow not just in numbers, but in spirit. Because "mi casa, su casa" isn't just about physical homes; it's about the Heart. About creating emotional homes for one another.

My Story: From Division to Devotion

I grew up in a family where loyalty to the birth family, particularly to the matriarchs, sometimes created painful divides. My father's allegiance remained tethered to his mother and sisters. My mother, though loved, often lived in the shadow of their influence. I saw the toll it took on her, and on another aunt who married into the same dynamic. From a young age, I knew this pattern would end with me.

I made a quiet vow: every person my children chose to be in partnership with, I would love and fully embrace as if they were my own children. Not because they are perfect, but because they are *their choice*.

That intention has shaped some of the most meaningful relationships of my life. It has made holidays more joyful. It has allowed us to blend traditions, share laughter, and hold each other's hands through change. We don't divide. We multiply.

One of the most tender confirmations of this came with the birth of my first grandson. My son and his wife, Laura, live in upstate New York near her family. I live across the country in Malibu. The morning of her delivery, my son called: "Today's the day." I dropped everything, rearranged my schedule, and caught the next flight east.

When I walked into her hospital room the next morning, Laura's mother hugged me tightly and smiled: "Congratulations, cool grandmas!"

It was more than a greeting. It was a **welcome**. In that moment, we stood together, not just as in-laws, but as equals. As family.

Before rushing to meet my son, cradling his newborn son, I first walked over to my daughter-in-law to check in, gently, and lovingly, after her C-section. Her eyes told the whole truth: the deep joy of new life and the raw pain of bringing it forth. Both lived there, side by side. I hugged her with so much love and appreciation for her 9 month journey and emotional delivery. I saw her strength.

When my son placed his baby in my arms and whispered, "Here you go, Mom, he's all yours," something shifted. I felt a love that transcended biology, boundaries, and names. It was sacred, unspoken, and infinite.

Later that week, they invited me to stay, not in a hotel, but in their home. And when Laura's parents left for their lake house, they entrusted me, without hesitation, to care for their daughter and our grandson. It was a gesture of pure trust, for all of us.

A few months later, Laura sent me a TikTok video, a sweet montage capturing my arrival at the hospital: a playful "cool grandma" hug with her mom, our emotional embrace, and the first time I held my grandson. The video gained unexpected traction, sparking conversations around the dynamics of mother-in-law and daughter-in-law relationships. The responses spanned the spectrum, from stories of deep appreciation and connection to painful tales of tension and distance. But beyond the comments and the reach, the video revealed something deeper: love, inclusion and sacred expansion.

That was the real story. And in that moment, watching it back, I realized this is all I ever wanted. Curious to watch the TikTok video? Search @thelifeoflauraaa.

How to Welcome In-Laws into Your Heart

Welcoming in-laws is more than politeness; it's a practice of love, inclusion, and expansion. It means choosing to soften where you might guard, to open where you've been conditioned to close. These relationships can become rich and meaningful when we approach them not with duty, but with intention and Heart.

Reflect

Begin by examining the beliefs, patterns, and emotional stories you may carry, consciously or unconsciously, around in-laws.

- What beliefs about in-laws did you inherit from your own family or culture?
- Were you taught to welcome them with warmth or to keep them at arm's length?
- How have your past experiences shaped your current openness or resistance to these relationships?

Journaling Prompt: *What assumptions or expectations do I hold about in-laws? Where might I have unknowingly created distance and what might I be protecting?*

Reframe

Rewriting the story around in-laws begins with shifting how we see them, not as extensions of someone else, but as whole people, worthy of their own space in our Hearts.

- An in-law is not an outsider, they are someone's beloved, someone's world.
- They are family, not by blood, but by choice and love.
- Every loving act toward them strengthens your family's foundation of trust, unity, and grace.

Empowering Question: *What would shift if I treated my in-laws not as guests in my life, but as family in the fullest sense of the word?*

Reconnect

Connection doesn't require perfection; it requires presence, intention, and small acts of generosity that build trust over time.

- Set a heartfelt intention for your relationship: How do I want to feel and help others feel when we're all together?
- Invite moments of shared humanity: a meal, a memory, a gesture of inclusion that says, "You belong here."
- Speak of them with kindness, especially to the next generation. Let your words plant seeds of unity.

Affirmation: *My Heart has room for more family. I choose warmth over walls, and presence over pride. I welcome love in all its forms.*

Final Thought: The Heart Has Room

Welcoming in-laws is expansion.
It is love widening its circle.
It is saying with sincerity,
there is room for you here.

Loving who our children love multiplies grace.
It heals what came before us.
It models openness, not ownership.
It turns family into belonging.

Family is not only blood.
Family is a shared presence.
It is laughter at new tables.
It is hands lifting one another.

Every welcome becomes a bridge.
Every inclusion becomes a legacy.
Warmth builds what walls cannot.
Love grows when we choose to share it.

This is Sovereign Living.

ACKNOWLEDGEMENTS

I'd like to acknowledge the many teachers I've met along the way, around the globe:

Soul Sisters
Kimberly Konstant, Business and Soulbbatical Travel Partner
Lisa Tenore, Yoga Teacher and Divinely Guided Intuitive

Book Co-Creation
Helane Freeman, Design & Layout
Mitch Sisskind, Editor
Sydney Koenig, Photography

Yoga-Mindful Teachers
Alexia Daksha Damini, Alice Khalsa, Bilge Alpay, Carla Fabre, Chrissy MJ Anderson, Christopher Tompkins, Colleen Lila Yoga, Elana Brower, Guru Jagat, Guru Jas Khalsa, Harijiwan, Harmanjot Kaur, Isa Raim, Parashakti, Philipp Manser, Ram Kirin, Raquel Griffin, Sarah Miller: Siri Akasha, Schuyler Grant, Shiva Rea, Susan Shaner, Teddy Dean, Tej Kaur Khalsa

Guides
Agus Sihman, Ama, Andrea Caresse, Ellen Goldberg, Ingo Alexander Sohn, Janet Schmidt, Jessica Kruskamp, June Fagan, Krista Polinsky, Nicole Rager, Saul, Taita, Tracy Mignon

Thought Leaders & Book Authors
Alan Watts, Barbara Waxman, Brene Brown, Bruce Feiler, Bruce Lipton, Carol Dweck, Chip Conley, Crystal and Mark Victor Hansen, Danielle LaPorte, David Kessler, Deepak Chopra, Dr. Gabor Maté,

Dr. Gary Chapman, Don Miguel Ruiz, Eckhart Tolle,
Elizabeth Gilbert, Esther Perel, Gabrielle Bernstein,
Gregg Braden, Haamid Dash, Helane Anderson,
Iyanla Vanzant, Jay Rubin, Jay Shetty, Joe Dispenza,
John Gray, Katherine Woodward Thomas,
Leigh and Carla McCloskey, Louise Hay,
Marie Forleo, Mark Nepo, Matthew McConaughey,
Mel Robbins, Michaela Boehm, Norma Kamali,
Paulo Coelho, Reverend Michael Bernard Beckwith,
Rhonda Byrne, Rich Roll, Rob Bell, Shelley Paxton,
Simon Sinek, Vishen Lakhiani and Wayne Dyer

A heartfelt thank you to **Chip Conley**, founder of Modern Elder Academy, and **Gerard Armond Powell**, founder of Rythmia Life Advancement Center.

In beautifully distinct yet equally transformative ways, you each became luminous guides on my journey toward intentional living. Though your paths differ in form, they meet in purpose: a shared devotion to helping others remember who they are and what they are here to become.

Through my years serving as Marketing Director within both of your worlds, I was given a rare privilege: a front-row seat to transformation in its purest form. Chip, your work at Modern Elder Academy reshaped how I view aging, purpose, and wisdom, revealing that elderhood is not a closing chapter but a profound awakening. Gerry, your vision at Rythmia illuminated the sacred union between healing and wholeness, reminding me that freedom begins when the Heart comes home to itself.

Your retreats, your teachings, and your unwavering belief in human potential each invited me into deeper truth. You inspired me to live more consciously, to love more courageously, and to help women everywhere reclaim their Sovereignty, their radiant and unshakable sense of self.

I carry the essence of both of your teachings within my own work, grateful for the intersection of grace, grit, and growth that our paths have shared. May we continue to meet in spaces of awakening, wherever Hearts gather to remember the sacred truth of who they are.

ABOUT THE AUTHOR

Laura Alfano is the visionary behind *Sovereign Living*, a movement to inspire 20 million women worldwide to reclaim their Crown, Heart and Compass, and to fully embody their power. Born and raised in Port Chester, New York, as the eldest of three, she grew up rooted in the values of faith, perseverance, and family. A natural achiever, she graduated high school early, earned her associate's degree in Fashion Merchandising, and went on to complete a bachelor's degree in Marketing and Management at Pace University.

After college, Laura married, welcomed three healthy children into the world, and raised them while simultaneously building a successful career in marketing with leading consumer packaged goods companies and creative agencies in the NY/CT area. She later transitioned into consulting to create a healthier balance for her family, carrying her instinct for beauty and design into every role she touched.

In 2007, Laura's life was forever altered by the sudden loss of her brother. What began in heartbreak set off a chain reaction of deeper pain and disappointment: the unraveling of her marriage and the painful estrangement from two of her children. Following her losses, Laura embarked on a spiritual journey of self-discovery, a season of exploration and awakening. As a devoted student, she traveled widely, studied various yoga lineages, read extensively in the fields of personal growth, and participated in transformational courses. Even an unplanned plant medicine journey became part of her path toward healing. Through this process, Laura reclaimed her Sovereignty, rediscovering her Crown of self-worth, her Heart of compassion, and her Compass of inner wisdom.

Today, Laura lives seaside in Malibu, California, delighting in her role as mother and grandmother. She is a Luxury Real Estate Advisor, a certified Hatha and Kundalini Yoga teacher and Reiki Master. Out of her personal journey, she created the *Sovereign Living* series of books, workbooks, and inspiration cards; resources designed to help women everywhere embody their worth and rise into lives of beauty, balance, joy, and Sovereignty.

DISCOVER THE SOVEREIGN LIVING COLLECTION

Continue your journey of self-discovery and empowerment with the complete *Sovereign Living* series. Alongside each book, you'll find a companion workbook to help you Reflect, Reframe, and Reconnect, plus a deck of inspiration cards to keep your practice alive every day. Choose one or embrace them all to reclaim your Crown, your Heart, and your Compass.

Sovereign Living I: A Woman's Guide to Reclaiming Your Crown

Sovereign Living I Workbook: Reclaiming Your Crown - Reflect, Reframe, Reconnect

Sovereign Living I Inspiration Cards: Reclaiming Your Crown

Sovereign Living II: A Woman's Guide to Reclaiming Your Heart

Sovereign Living II Workbook: Reclaiming Your Heart - Reflect, Reframe, Reconnect

Sovereign Living II Inspiration Cards: Reclaiming Your Heart

Sovereign Living III: A Woman's Guide to Reclaiming Your Compass

Sovereign Living III Workbook: Reclaiming Your Compass - Reflect, Reframe, Reconnect

Sovereign Living III Inspiration Cards: Reclaiming Your Compass

Workbooks and Inspiration Cards coming as soon as 2026

www.ingramcontent.com/pod-product-compliance
Lightning Source LLC
Chambersburg PA
CBHW041216130526
44582CB00025BA/37